The Pigs' Slaughter

Florin Grancea

ISBN: 145638239X
ISBN-13: 978-1456382391

As a narrative nonfiction the contents
of this work fall under the protection offered by the First
Amendment

◎   The front cover picture was first published in "1989 Libertate
Roumanie" by Denoel Paris (ISBN 2-207-23695-1)

TO

My kids, Mihai (4) and Angela (2) who are lucky to be born and raised in a free country, to Mayo, my beloved wife, to my mother who raised me well in a time of struggle and to my father, who always protected us and saw things that, at the time, we did not.

CONTENTS

ACKNOWLEDGMENTS

I wrote this book in two weeks under pressure from my dearest friend Nathan O'Neill. As a many-time guest for dinner, Nathan was always delighted with my Romanian stories and repeatedly asked me to write them down. I did, and having started I raced to the end with him at my side as a Mr. Watson of proofreading. Without his support, this book may not have been written at all.

1. DECEMBER 21ST

The truth is that I was slaughtering the pig.

When the Romanian Revolution started and people rushed to overturn Ceaușescu, or rushed to sit in front of their TV sets and watch how people were slaughtered on the streets of Timișoara, Bucharest and Sibiu, I was rushing a knife into a pig.

The previous day was Ignat's Day, pig slaughtering day in Romania. We were one day late. My Unitra (Polish made) radio was turned on loud tuned to Radio Free Europe. Until a couple of days earlier we could only listen to it after dark, and with the volume turned down. To listen to it in the open would have meant beatings, jail time or even death.

Was I stupid? Maybe, but I didn't care anymore. News from Timișoara said that there were thousands and thousands of deaths, so it had to be over soon.

I rushed to spread the news. The good news: the Revolution continued!

"Daaad!" My voice straining, my heartbeat quickening, I rushed into the backyard.

The pig was there, my dad was there, Uncle Lulu was there, too, sipping hot wine from a mug.

"Where the hell have you been? You're holdin' up the show", said my dad, like I was about to miss all the fun.

His friend, Mr. Brana, was taking the role of butcher. He had a rather small knife in his hand, pointed with a thin and narrow blade. It didn't have a blood gutter.

It always takes three people to slaughter a pig. Two won't do, four are always too many. That's why Uncle Lulu was on the hot wine. At 7:00 in the morning, the hot wine was a better choice than a mug of coffee. It was cold out. Really cold.

Now you could tell that the pig was nervous. These animals that we eat on Christmas day are smarter than dogs and it could see it coming. My father had the rope, Mr. Brana, the knife...

"Get the bucket ready, will you?"

A last minute instruction from my dad.

To slaughter a pig you need a knife, a rope and a bucket. Nothing more, nothing less.

The tension was mounting. We closed the gate of the small backyard to make the job of catching the pig easier, and the pig didn't like it. I have heard stories of pigs attacking their would-be slaughterers and mauling them to death, and certainly some crazy pigs were capable of it. Maybe that was the reason my fingers were trembling as I held the bucket... Maybe it was the news on the radio.

Well, we had a job to do and the news had to wait.

My father approached the pig with the rope and using his hand started to rub the pig's head. Pigs like that. I have seen some fall asleep, and even fall flat in a matter of seconds, from a good head rub.

Well, this particular beast didn't fall asleep. It was too smart to sleep through its last minutes of life, but for some reason touched its head on my dad's leg. Affection? Fear? Both?

The rope had a sliding knot in it and my father let the pig step into it. Its left front leg was trapped but it didn't realize it. Yet. For the pig this was a wrong move. Now it was almost over. My dad pulled the rope, the pig went down and, like a wrestler, my dad put his weight down on it, holding it down.

If I had been any younger, I would have rode it too. Kids always ride the pigs while they are being slaughtered. But now I was fourteen and I was replacing my mother with the bucket. My sister never rode the pigs. She couldn't see a life being taken, not even a pig's life.

"Son, be ready with that", Mr. Brana said in a hushed voice. He threw his unfinished cigarette in the snow. A rectangular hole with some smoke rising out of it appeared near my feet. Then, he got close to my wrestling dad, and waited for me.

As soon as I had the bucket ready he put his left hand on the pig's head and with his right he thrust his knife into the pig's neck. I don't know if you have ever slaughtered a pig, or even had the chance to see one being slaughtered close up. But you can easily imagine it by realizing how similar our anatomy and the pig's are.

A 150kg live pig doesn't look like much. Four legs, fat, with a wide back. The head seems to be attached directly onto the body. It only seems so. Its neck is there.

Feel your own neck! The base of it at the front...You can feel where the chest bone begins. Less than 20cm below that point is your heart. Less than 20cm below that point on the pig is the pig's heart too.

Mr. Brana thrust his knife into the pig's neck aiming for the heart. Professionals always aim for the heart. Only drunk or dumb people try to behead the pig when they slaughter it. Ridiculous. The fat around the pig's neck can be very tricky and it is not nice being around an injured animal that outweighs you twice-over.

The knife goes in and comes out. The blood spurts out in a thick jet stream. The previous year I wasn't ready and the first of the blood sprayed a wall - 6 meters away. But I was ready this time. The blood started to fill the bucket. There would be about 5 liters in all. Even after the pig stops moving, its heart, or what is left of it, continues to pump blood out of the body. The vicious eyes of the animal calm down and look back at you, sympathetic. A moment later they glaze over.

"Take the blood to your mom", Mr. Brana spoke in a professional air, with no sign of the kick of adrenaline he had just had while killing the pig. The blood I collected would be the main ingredient in "sângerete", the blood sausages which would be our only source of iron over the winter.

In Romania spinach starts growing in early April, so, without blood sausages a body will, sooner or later, be afflicted by a severe case of anemia - it was better to be with them than without them. Our precious blood for the winter...

My mom filtered the blood for whatever impurities it might have had and transferred it into a pot. She would add salt, black pepper and herbs and stir it on the fire until the future sausages became soot black and thick paste. Then she would wait.

I, too, was waiting for something. The public broadcast. Ceaușescu had returned the previous day from Iran. I didn't know it and he didn't know it either, but the Iran affair was to be his last trip abroad, only five days prior to his death. But hey, to imagine Ceaușescu dead in December '89 was like imagining Santa was real. That public broadcast was supposed to show a huge demonstration in support of Ceaușescu and we all hoped that something would happen. Maybe he would step down, maybe he would heed the protests and loosen his grip on us, anything could happen and I was going to watch it.

Back in the backyard it was the same group. Only now the pig was dead. A white pig on white snow, Uncle Lulu sipping the hot wine, my dad and Mr. Brana smoking their stinky Romanian-made cigarettes. It was a time when Japanese, British and even Turkish tobacco brands were sold on the black market only. You could buy one pack of 20 cigarettes for a doctor so he would anesthetize you before cutting you open, but never to smoke on the grand occasion of slaughtering your pig.

The silence was deafening. The few dozen chickens and roosters we kept turned quiet in their roosts. They understood that something "bad" had just happened, or they had smelled the blood I had collected, or...I really don't know, nor quite give a shit, but they were silent too.

Despite being 14 at the time I got myself a mug of hot wine and took a long sip. It was hot and sweet. Mine was over boiled so it had little or no alcohol. Just the way I liked it. My mom brought some hot brandy for Mr. Brana and my dad, a home made plum spirit, 55% alcohol, boiled with black pepper. Our outdoor party had to continue despite the freezing temperatures we had in Avrig, and the booze was the answer to Mr. Brana's prayers.

"Boy, get the straw ready ", Mr. Brana addressed me again, and I put my mug down and headed for the barn. Climbed the ladder to where the wheat straw was stored and pushed down the equivalent in volume of a large Japanese goose dove futon. I climbed down and took half of it and spread it over the dead pig.

The pig was on its back, now, and my father helped it stay on its back with two bricks pushed against its body on both sides. When ready, I took a matchbox, opened it, took out a match, lit it and a moment later the pig was on fire. A few minutes later the fire was out and Mr. Brana and my father turned the pig on its belly and I burned it again with the remaining straw. Time for another mug of hot wine for me and Uncle Lulu and another shot of hot brandy for my father and Mr. Brana.

"Help me with that door", my father said and we took down the barn door and lay it on the snow. Beside it was the charred and dead pig resting in an anthracite black spot where the snow had been melted by the fire.

The three of us (my father, Mr. Brana and I) took the pig by its legs and pushed it onto the door. Uncle Lulu went to the kitchen to hurry my mother with the hot water: the boys were about to give the pig a close shave. The straw fire burned the hairs and dead cells off the pig's skin, so we had to literally shave it, using hot water and sharp knives. But first we had to clean it with hot water and brushes, which we did.

In less than an hour the charred looking pig had turned into an appetizing pink dream. I say dream because it was a time when eating meat was an extravagance in Romania. It was

December and I had last tasted the forbidden swine in early summer. Every Saturday I had killed a chicken or a rooster for Sunday lunch and supper, but not for the last month and a half. It was the Christmas fasting period: beans, beans, cabbage and then more beans. Just seeing the dead pig made me excited at the thought of suppers to come.

Anyway, the pig was cleaner than a groom on his wedding day, so Mr. Brana went for the first cut: he chopped its ears off and handed them to me. I took them with delight. A quick move with the knife and my trophy grew bigger with a 15" size notebook piece of skin.

In few seconds later in the kitchen I saw my mom slicing the skin and the ears and taking half of them upstairs to my sister. It was our snack for the unexpected public broadcast. Kids always eat the pig's ears. Raw. At least in Avrig they do, I'm not sure about kids in other counties. The Bucharest demonstration in support of Ceauşescu was about to begin and, strangely, it was to be aired before noon. We decided that we better watch it. Why? Who cared? Maybe nobody, not me, probably because at the time TV broadcasts amounted to a mere 2 hours of news about Ceauşescu, from 7:00pm to 9:00pm every day.

The patriotic songs and a computer generated image gave way to the image of a packed square and the building of the Central Committee of the Romanian Communist Party. Ceauşescu was doing his usual blah, blah, blah, promising a 100 lei increase in all salaries, about 4USD, despite the fact that all the stores were empty, with no goods to buy. Students were promised 10 lei more, or 40 US cents.

Listening to the fire in the terracotta stove I dipped a slice of raw pig ear in salt and put it in my mouth, savoring the moment, but before chewing it I jumped to my feet and screamed. On the TV screen there were images of other screams. Years later I learned that while I was eating the pig's ears, someone in the crowd shouted "Jos, Ceauşescu!" or "Down with Ceauşescu", and the rattling of guns or maybe just firecrackers were heard. The crowd started to run, the TV station tried to cut off the transmission but they cut the image feed only. We could still hear the Ceauşescus' fearful voices. They were scared!

75% of the population of Romania was in front of their TVs, like me and my sister. The other 25% were either on the streets, shouting "Jos, Ceauşescu" or slaughtering their pigs, like my parents, Mr. Brana and Uncle Lulu.

"Hello, hello", the brain-dead voice of the god-like former shoemaker blared in the speakers while his wife threw fuel on the fire advising him publicly:

"Talk to them, talk to them".

It was popularly believed that Ceauşescu wasn't so bad, but – as in many Romanian households – he was under the control of his wife. To have the proof of that feared reality was to provoke even more hysteria.

Like two broken puppets Ceauşescu and his wife stood there bewildered at what was going on. Why had they called the demonstration? Why had they given orders for the bloody backlash in Timişoara?

"Stay quietly where you are" tried Ceauşescu again, before being rushed into the building by his underlings. And the live feed was cut and replaced again with patriotic music. According to Radio Free Europe a third of the citizens of Timişoara had been killed. Way too many for Ceauşescu to get away with it by offering 100 lei more in monthly earnings for us Romanians.

With my mouthful of raw pig's ears I rushed into the backyard to tell the news.

Dad, it's happening, the people in Bucharest have started a revolt", I shouted overjoyed.

Mr. Brana froze, Uncle Lulu froze, and my dad froze too. I was so loud maybe the neighbors had heard it too.

"We still have to work on this pig", said my father, his words double edged, while my mother rushed with the hot wine and hot brandy again.

"I just hope the fucking Russians don't invade us" said my father, and I remembered how impressed he was when he visited Hungary, the one and only foreign country he had been to, when he saw the traces of the Soviet bullets on the beautiful buildings of Budapest. Their 1956 revolt was crushed by Soviet tanks and as a father he feared for us.

"You're right, man, we still have to work on this pig", echoed Mr. Brana, whatever the real meaning of his words were.

When I gave them the news he was about to cut off the pig's legs. The pig was on its belly, bricks positioned on either side of it, so he went to work on it surgically. First all four feet were chopped off and laid aside. My mom would salt them and hang them in the smokehouse. Then the legs followed. One hind leg was put in salt immediately. Four days in salt and then 1 month in the smokehouse, and then hung up to dry further. This was the method of choice for the best meat we could consume raw. The other three legs went into the kitchen where my mom started to take the meat off of them. With a small knife she cut off the fat and threw it into a bucket, the resulting fat-trimmed meat would go into another one. Two buckets full, another two to go, I carried the full buckets into the cold room and locked everything down. Our cats and dog were prowling around, waiting for a treat. If we were careless they would grab everything and this could never happen. The meat was more precious than their lives and I cared more about my family and our food supply than I cared for them.

Another two buckets in the cold room and I had to help my father put the fatback in salt.

Imagine the pig, now, with no legs. The next task was to cut the fat off the carcass. Mr. Brana made a long cut from the neck to the tail, and then cut off the back of the pig in two wide and heavy pieces. It is called "slănínă" in Romanian and it is mostly fatback. We do not remove the skin. These pieces are heavy and they have to withstand hanging on hooks for many months.

I took the meat down into the basement and put it on a table. I put several kilos of salt on one strip and then covered it with the other strip covering that with salt again. The salt would suck the water out of it, helping to preserve it. I know that the meat industry injects salt water and shit into meat products to make them weigh more in order to deceive clueless customers, but this was not our way of doing it. We loved our food, our natural food.

Back in the backyard the pig's head was cut off. After being washed and smashed to get at the brains – a delicacy children love to eat – it went into a big pot to be boiled. Its meat and cartilage would fill the pig's stomach and become what is known as "tobă", a heavy spicy sausage.

It was time, so Mr. Brana took a butcher knife and cut the pig's spine in two. Opened like this the body revealed its insides to us. The short knife collected for my mom the lungs, liver, kidneys, and the damaged heart. All of which went into a pot to be boiled. The stomach and the intestines went into a bucket to be washed in the river, and the bladder, washed with water, was cut in pieces and fed to the cats and dogs. It was the only part of the pig that we did not use.

It was before 2:00 pm when my mom gathered us around the table for the pig's funeral feast. Like in real funerals, after burying a beloved, people gather to share food and drinks in remembrance. We had to have a ceremony for our pig as well. Lovely and welcomed it was, because we could eat the meat without sinning, four or five days before Christmas! The pig's ears were meat, too, but somehow the rules were not as strict when applied to them. Only a couple of ears are not a big deal, and I never saw a pig with more than two.

For the feast, boneless red meat was fried with onions, sweet paprika, pepper and salt. After six weeks on beans and cabbage it was, served with homemade fresh bread, an angel's feast. Of course, empty glasses were quickly refilled and the euphoria – mainly the one that had to be suppressed in the past – could be expressed with conviction and hope. Fourteen years old, holding a plate of meat, a mug of hot wine in hand, in a kitchen crowded with half-drunk people and buckets full of meat, bones and fat, it was the first, and I suspect the last, time that I was really proud of being Romanian.

The son of a proud nation that was fighting for its freedom, I was celebrating our nation of people who had balls. I didn't pity those who died in Timișoara, not one single one of them. They

died for freedom, they were heroes, and they had certainly bigger
balls than I had at the time. We had prayed for the pig when we
ate its meat. Now, because the feast was over and we had to
make at least 4 kinds of sausages by nightfall, we had to pray
again.

"Thank you Lord for this pig that you brought to our table.
Thank you Lord for taking care of us. Take care also of those
who left this cruel world these last days at the hands of
communists, and keep us safe, keep the Russian pigs away from
our country, don't let them come to crush us in our motherland
nest", my father finished and emptied his glass on the ground.
Mr. Brana said "Amen" and emptied his glass as well on the
kitchen floor. It was customary to empty one's glass on the
ground for the last toast. The souls of the dead had to drink too.

My mom had removed the carpet in the early hours of the
morning and the place was already quite dirty and, anyway, it
didn't matter.

My father took a knife and cut two blocks of good meat. One
for Mr. Brana, for helping us and one for Uncle Lulu, for sipping
the hot wine with us. In a starving country where people were
risking their lives to overturn the dictator there wasn't a more
appreciated present.

More drinks and they went home. With an ear for Radio Free
Europe, we started to mince the meat, onions and garlic. We had
two mincing machines. One that my grandmother got as a
wedding present in 1921, and another that my mother got as a
wedding present in 1974. I could tell that the one from before
WWII was better but, because it was bigger, my father had it to
himself.

"The citizens are taking to the streets and the army is using
machine guns on them", the passionate report that we heard on
the radio made us stop for a second.

"We have to win", "the pig must go down", my father said
furious and increased the speed of the mincing machine. At that
point my granny returned with the washed stomach and
intestines. Actually "washed" is a kind word for what happened

to them. Of course she had washed them, but washing them was just the start of a long and laborious procedure. First she emptied them. Now, if you have to do this inside be forewarned that it is a stinky procedure. But out in the open air and at minus 10 degrees centigrade it is not so bad. Then she washed them in clean water, and rubbed them in salt. Finally she took a blunt knife and pulled them between its blunt blade and a polished wooden block so that all the interior walls were ejected. In the end only the transparent exterior membrane remained. This was rubbed in salt again, and again washed, and rubbed in salt again and then washed again, until it lost its odour. The same procedures were applied to the small and big intestines, and even harsher treatment for the stomach.

It was about time to fill them up. Before it got dark, and before my father got drunk. The big intestine became the membrane for "caltabosh", a specialty made from the head's meat, lungs, kidneys and heart. The small intestine was divided between the meat sausages, the liver pate and the "sângerete" and the blood sausages. All the other small cuts of meat and head cartilages went into the pig's stomach to become the highly prized "tobă", which is also the Romanian word for drum.

It was suddenly night outside and we were bloody tired. The meat sausages went into the smokehouse. All the other specialties followed after first being boiled. I made the fire. I used the customary willow wood and willow wood sawdust to cover the fire. That was the best smoke I could imagine for our fresh sausages.

We stayed up to clean the kitchen floor, scrub it with brushes and rinse it with hot water. The next morning my mom would put the carpet back, but that had to wait until the next morning. Soon after my father called it a day.

And what a day it had been! I was full of meat, the first time in many months, my house was warm and outside, in the snow, the willow smoke was coming out of the smokehouse like a surreal fog. The present was foggy but with signs of prosperity visible, and going to sleep the night before I really hoped for a more prosperous tomorrow.

"Dad!" I whispered from my room...

"What? Go to sleep," his answer came through the door that was separating our bedrooms.

"If Ceaușescu falls, what's gonna happen?"

My question hung in the air, frozen for many minutes.

"We will be free!"

I could sense the emotions running deep within my father's thoughts. Free. Like an echo, the word bounced back and forth inside my head. Free. Wasn't I free at that very moment? Was I in a kind of prison? Free...

I was rebelling like all 14-year-old rebels, so wasn't I free? Wasn't my dad free? Because we lived in a house and not in an apartment. We were required to give, according to the rules, a pig, our pig, to our motherland. Our motherland was fucking hungry and wanted to eat our pig. But we just slaughtered it for ourselves. Because we had no grain and no potatoes to raise two pigs...And we never fucking gave our pigs to our motherland! We did have choices, didn't we? We lived in a communist country and we lived in fear, but for some reason I didn't think of myself as not being free.

I rolled over under the heavy woolen duvet and fell asleep. I was free. I was going to be free. My last vivid memory of that 21st of December was the willow smoke perfume lingering on my dirty fingers.

As it happens, the perfume of smoke was Jean Louis Calderon's last vivid memory too. As I drifted off he was being killed near the Intercontinental Hotel in Bucharest, one block away from the soon to be renamed, Jean Louis Calderon Street. That street, that area must have felt familiar to him, as the buildings there resembled his very own Paris and the neighborhood around Liberation headquarters, but he never imagined these streets going under French names.

As a Frenchman he knew what was unfolding before his eyes and why he was there. Vive la Révolution!

In 1789 his countrymen and women took to the streets to fight against tyranny. Liberté, Égalité, Fraternité were becoming so palpable, so real. "Fraternité" was the key word and that was why he refused to watch the events from the safety of the Intercontinental Hotel, like all the Anglo-Saxon journalists. So there he was, on the street, surrounded by tanks and soldiers. People shouting, guns rattling, a barricade being raised like back in 1789 and then being attacked. And defended. And conquered. And it was that girl that he saw, happy and beautiful, facing the bullets and he wanted to be like her, wanted to get to know her and wanted to remember her forever. But smoke was the last thing he was able to think of. Jean Louis Calderon died in an anti-climax to his own exciting life of storytelling.

2. DECEMBER 22ND

Waking up on December 22nd I didn't think about Jean Louis Calderon. I didn't know him and his story, and, even 5 years later, when I was myself an apprentice journalist running to press conferences held in some French-looking buildings on Jean Louis Calderon Street, it never crossed my mind that the street was named after a journalist.

Unlikely. Maybe a composer or a painter that everyone but me knows. That had to be it. That was the non-story that Jean Louis Calderon Street told.

As it happens, my dad took a day off on that 22nd of December. It was Friday and it had nothing to do with the pig. "If something happens it's better not to be there", he said to my mom when she left at 6:30 for her job. She had a job in a glass factory that employed half of my town's population. The other half was employed at Marsa Mechanical, a factory hidden in the woods that made huge dump trucks and armored military vehicles. My father had worked for both, but he got bored and changed his job to one that gave him freedom. So, on that

December 22nd he was head of the Civil Defense in Avrig, my tiny Transylvanian town.

As a matter of fact nobody else worked with him in the Civil Defense. The Civil Defense was a nonexistent department in the Town Hall, created maybe because Ceaușescu had had a bad dream once in Bucharest.

"I have to think about measures for times when floods, fires and earthquakes happen. Also hiding places for when the Russians decide to bomb us", he once told me.

"But we never have floods, fires or earthquakes here," I replied. "And there is nowhere to hide here, I never heard of shelters in Avrig". My reply made him laugh:

"That's why I took this job".

He had to report to the military, now and then, and the military, in the person of "The Colonel" started to attend our picnics on Sunday. They were a nice family from Cisnadie, one that we kept in touch with even after my dad had gone to meet Jean Louis Calderon.

But of course that was something I didn't know that morning. News like from another world blared from the radio. Radio Free Europe was informing us that Ceaușescu's days were numbered. There was a Revolution happening in Romania, a bloody revolution, and Romanians were united and standing against their "beloved" dictator.

I could tell my father was afraid. Expectant and afraid. As an employee of the Town Hall he WAS the fucking state! Why did he have to change his job? He had nothing to fear as a technician with Marsa Mechanical, but that wasn't the situation anymore.

"Go and get the smoke going, or we ain't gonna eat sausages this year", my father ordered. "Then, come back to the kitchen, we still have work to do".

The willow I got that year was so dry that it took me less than a minute to make the fire. I watched it for a few moments while I warmed my hands. The fire was in a large bucket placed right beneath our sausages, caltaboshi, pate and toba. They all looked cold, with traces of fat dripping from last night. I had to be quicker. The smokehouse wasn't supposed to be hot. Minus temperatures were preferred. I took a bag of willow sawdust and poured it onto the fire. The secret was to use just enough to keep the fire going beneath it and produce smoke. If I poured more than just enough, the fire would go out and there would be no smoke. If I poured less than just enough, the fire would eat through the sawdust and burn with open flames, something which we had to avoid. The meats would surely rot if warm.

I was satisfied with my work and looked at my watch making a mental note. Every hour I had to come back to pour more sawdust into the bucket. I went to the door, and then, kicking the cat to stop the hungry animal from getting in, I went out and locked the smokehouse door behind me. It wasn't unheard of that thieves, especially gypsies, would steal people's sausages at night or in broad daylight, so I had to be careful. Only a couple of days before, when my neighbors got up to slaughter their pig for Ignat's Day, they discovered it gone. Three empty bottles of beer had been dropped where the pig was, and the Militia man said: "Smart, they took it while you were asleep so you wouldn't hear anything", but then he added, "If you find out who the thieves are, inform us straightaway so we can arrest them", and he hurried away because he, too, had a pig to kill. At that moment, my entire family was counting on me and I was going to do it right.

"Well done!" My father said to me when I entered the kitchen. From the window he could see the smoke rising from under the heavy snow that covered the roof of the smokehouse. He didn't know, and neither did I, but it was the last winter we would see that roof. The following spring we knocked the smokehouse and rebuilt it beside the barn. My mom wanted more space for flowers in the front yard and the smokehouse stood in her way.

Breakfast was rye bread, beans, pickles and zacusca, a Romanian version of ratatouille, over-boiled so we used it as a spread. I wolfed it down in big mouthfuls. My grandmother entered the kitchen with a big frying pan. My dad brought a heavy wooden board from outside and his butcher knife. I finished my meal quickly. Felicia, my sister, had already taken her breakfast upstairs to eat it in our room.

Now, that the table was clean, my dad set half of the pig's ribs on it and he started to separate them with a sharp knife. I helped. One hour we worked in silence. After we were done we put the separated ribs in two empty and clean buckets and placed them back in the pantry.

He came back with the other half of the pig's ribs and then fixed a drink and lit a cigarette. It was time for me to go and check the news. The TV was upstairs with my sister.

"Romanians, remain in front of your TV sets! An important communiqué for the Nation will soon follow!"

As soon as I entered the room I heard the announcement. The voice from the black & white Opera TV set was reproducing a stereotypical message from war movies about the 23rd of August, 1944, the day Romania changed sides in the war and started to fight against the Germans. Making friends with the fucking Russians wasn't a choice I supported, nor understood. As a Junior High School student, then in my last year, I was quite opinionated and called all ugly teachers and students – not that there were many – "as beautiful as the Russian language".

It all started with my grandfather who had told me how in the First World War and then again in the Second World War our house was commandeered by Germans, and how the Germans were civilized, didn't leave dirty toilets behind and how they paid a fair price for what they got.

"But not the Russians!" he always said with clenched fists. The story was that when the Russian soldiers came, they took all of his tomatoes, apples and chickens, and when he asked for money they fired their guns over his head and punched him to the ground. A few days later, when more Russians came, his coat and his watch were taken. And his wine too. Then, in the cold spring of 1945, when his house was commandeered by an officer, the soviet bastard wanted to rape his daughter. My Aunt Anişoara was 13 in '45, and my grandfather used his Colt Revolver to protect her. He told me that he pushed the officer for 3 kilometers with the gun, and let him run away only after they were far away from our village. He couldn't kill the man, and he hoped he wouldn't be able to come back, wouldn't be able to tell which village it was.

So it goes that my grandfather lived year after year with the fear that that particular officer would come back, from Berlin or from Moscow, to take revenge for the night spent in the unknown woods. That was the story.

All this came back to me like a flash in my mind. I was already rushing downstairs with the news. Who could have known then that I was destined to make a living from producing and selling news in the future? Not me. Back in December 1989 I was thinking of becoming a doctor in the future. Doctors always had money, they were respected and they were maybe the only profession that didn't have to applaud Ceaușescu. We all had to clap for our dictator on important occasions, such as his visits, school year opening ceremonies, graduation parties and the like.

"Dad, it's over! Ceaușescu is finished!" I shouted at my dad, as I entered the kitchen, and he stood up and came and hugged me.

"That's the best news I've ever heard", he said delighted, poured a drink and went to the phone. He sounded so happy and acted like we had just won the lottery, but the anxiety and fear never left his eyes.

Phone calls to my mom – she said that people in the glass factory were getting ready to march to take over the Town Hall – to friends and relatives. It was like New Year's night when he called everyone for New Year's greetings.

"We should get the ribs ready for the lard". It was my grandmother, insensible as always to political situations but very much sensitive to food issues.

The ribs had to be cut in pieces 5cm long and salted and then deep fried in lard. Then they had to be placed in 5 liter jars and covered in lard. The lard would solidify into a bright white color. Here and there a cinnamon brown shadow reveals it's a meat jar and not merely a lard jar. Then, everyday, my mom would take a greasy fried piece of rib and put it in a pan, fry it with chopped onion and garlic. This is how all cooking begins in Romania, it doesn't matter what the desired dish is. The vegetables chosen and subsequent preparations make the difference.

Chop. Chop.

The butcher knife went up and down, up and down, cutting the ribs with precision. My grandmother was readying the 5 liter glass jars and heating the fry pan. After my dad is done it would be her job to finish and preserve the ribs.

With nothing left to do in the kitchen I went to see my fire and add sawdust to the smokehouse's bucket. Then I was back upstairs, where my sister was already sitting comfortably in the front of the TV.

I didn't know at the time, but most of my countrymen spent their Revolution watching TV. Somehow the TV crews that were supposed to transmit another attempt by Ceauşescu to calm the people by speaking to the crowds started to broadcast live images of the revolt. The very large square in front of the Central Committee of the Romanian Communist Party was packed with people attacking the infamous building. It was our Bastille, but Jean Louis Calderon was already dead and didn't see it fall. Those tortured and killed by the Secret Police in its basements in the aftermath of communist power being installed in Romania at the end of WWII, didn't see it either. Maybe some of them could have foreseen today's events, but I'm sure that they never imagined that almost all their countrymen would stay at home, watch TV, sip drinks and pat each other on the back.

"Let's go into town and see what's happening". It was my sister Felicia, as usual, coming up with a crazy idea.

"Are you nuts?" I asked and didn't wait for her reply. My dad was about to enter the room, the only one with a TV set back then, and he had overheard her proposal.

"I forbid you to go outside the gate. The gate will stay closed until I say so", went my dad, with unexpected calmness. Then he put down the tray he was carrying, two mugs of hot cocoa for us and a hot coffee for him.

Sipping our drinks we watched with enthusiasm how people entered the Central Committee building, how they threw things from the balcony where Ceauşescu last stood, how they were trying to address us, the people watching and encouraging them.

"God forbid the Russians come", my father was worrying when my mom entered the room. She was all purple and radiating with joy. I guess she never completely understood what was going on, but the general idea was: we had to be happy it was over.

What was over and what was about to begin were things we couldn't even grasp.

"What is freedom?" My question was raised again but this time my father answered without thinking.

"Freedom is when you can do whatever you like to do without the pig Ceauşescu there to stop you".

A few years later I was in a train headed for the Black Sea coast. It was crowded and people had to stand in the aisles. There were bags everywhere, sweat and a metallic taste in people's mouths. It was hot. Very hot. So first I didn't quite understand what was happening when all of a sudden, a group of youngsters started to break doors and seats. The toilet door came off first and they opened the carriage doors and dropped it out, all laughing. Knives in hand, they attacked any appliances that could be removed or destroyed while everybody watched in fear.

"Why are you doing this?" an old man asked them visibly hurt by what he was seeing and he got an answer that echoed my father's:

"Shut the fuck up, old fart. Maybe you didn't notice but Ceauşescu's gone. There's democracy in Romania and we are free!" Bang! Bang! The train's toilet, a dirty one, flew out of the water closet and then out of the speeding train. The youngsters were right, after all. They were free...

From the blaring TV set we could hear people chanting: "We are the people, down with the dictator", "Ole, ole, Ceauşescu is no more", "Freedom, freedom" and the like. And we saw the flag. The communist coat of arms cut out and the flag had a hole in its middle yellow stripe.

I jumped up and took my grandfather's flag, one with no hole in it, but with no communist coat of arms either, and I hung it outside the front door where it could be seen from the street. I was so proud. My grandfather had had that flag since 1918. He was 14 when Transylvania became, at the end of WWI, a part of Romania, and people from his village marched with handmade Romanian flags to Alba Iulia where they proclaimed their will for unity.

"Dad, let me see what's happening at the Town Hall", my sister pleaded again.

"No, please think", my dad replied. "It might get dangerous. Some people might shoot their guns and usually it's innocent bystanders that get killed", he said, with the experience of listening to the real world's news offered by Radio Free Europe and Voice of America.

"I am the one that should go", he continued, "and I would be more relaxed if I knew you were all safe here".

"Yes, sir!" All we could do was obey and respect his decision. It was his call, not ours.

My mom asked if we wanted something, anything, and said she would go help my grandmother with the ribs. I said nothing. I wasn't exactly delighted with my dad's decision, and I went downstairs to put some more sawdust on the willow smoking fire. Maybe my sister was right and we were just wasting a good chance to see something happening in that town where usually nothing happened.

I was about to lock the smokehouse behind me when I heard them. Since the gate had to stay closed at all times I rushed not to the gate but upstairs, from where I could see the street. When I arrived my sister was already there, expectantly, eyes gaping wide.

Two MLI armored personnel carriers, maybe the last two to ever be finished at Marsa Mechanical, were passing by. On them were people we knew, guns in hand, bottles in hand. They were happy and shouting. They were on their way to Sibiu, to help the Revolution. It was the first time for me to see armored vehicles actually being driven. Usually I saw them covered under military camouflage sheets, loaded on big trailers while they were shipped out of our town.

They looked crazy and beautiful, and half of me feared them and the other half envied the people driving them. A few seconds after they passed I heard the boom. And the bang, and then all the swearwords the Romanian language can muster, in all possible combinations. My sister turned red.

What had happened was that the second armored vehicle had taken a corner too tightly and crashed into the Barna's house. That was the fourth house up from ours, the other three being the Olog's, David's and David's.

The Barna's house it was and that military machine with all its ammunition stayed pinned in there more than two weeks, well after the Revolution was over. People from the first vehicle wanted to pull it out, but after hours of trying and failing they said they should go to help in Sibiu anyway.

"Help what?" their wives were shouting from the small crowd of Revolution lovers that had gathered around the poor Barna's house. The Revolution started in a very unfortunate way for him, but, although he was unaware of it, in a few years the entrepreneurial freedom the Revolution brought would turn him into a well-off business man.

"Help what?", the echo turned into engines roaring. The "Revolutionaries" got into or climbed onto the MLI, all very drunk, with no exception.

That day the people in Sibiu were fortunate. Although many were killed around the military garrison, the drunken revolutionaries never made it to their city. They were stopped by a wise military patrol and ordered back to Marsa Mechanical: they were driving a military vehicle with no army markings!

I was following my father onto the street to see the MLI that had gotten stuck in the Barna's house but I only got a glimpse of it. He ordered me back inside our front yard and, reluctantly, I followed his order. Almost all old Transylvanian houses look like small fortresses, and despite ours having more garden space around it, a heavy gate separated us from the rest of the world. We could easily withstand a siege if karma turned someone or something against us.

The front yard was deep in snow. The trees were white with icicles. Breathtaking. I stood there for a long time waiting for my father to come back inside and ask him about the accident. Eventually I got cold and took a leak. It was fascinating to see the yellow urine melting the snow, creating a deep crevasse in it. I smiled. My folks would go crazy (again) after seeing the "evidence" left behind by the animal they were feeding. We always had guests, friends or relatives, twice a day or even more often. Now that Christmas was just about here, we could expect even more people dropping in. The thought of it made my silly leak look more shameful than it was, so the moment my father entered the gate I stamped my foot into the snow to cover my dirtiness. What a trained animal I was.

At first, my father said nothing, as we were walking toward the kitchen. The kitchen and the bathroom were separated from the rest of the house and we used the back door to get to them. The smell of the fried meat my mother was preparing got stronger as we got closer.

"Let's have some ribs with white bread", my father said, suddenly hurrying me towards the kitchen.

I could have easily fainted as I entered the kitchen. Four large glass jars were lined up and my mother was already filling one with fried ribs. On the stove in the biggest frying pan that we had, other ribs were changing color to cinnamon brown, the meat retreating towards the bones.

"I'll have two. With sour cabbage", I told mom.

When it came to food, I wasn't polite to her. As the young man of the house I was imitating my father who used few words to ask for food or drink. It took me many years to get rid of that habit, and even now, at 34, when back home I still expect her to fetch me water or bread when I need more.

Sitting down, my father started to devour the lard-fried ribs and bread and talk about the armored vehicle that had crashed near us. My mom was taking it seriously. She was white - she usually was - but now she was whiter and scared.

"The Marsa Mechanical workers are marching. They'll be here in a few minutes. I'm going with them", my father said almost whispering.

"No, you can't do that, you have to stay here with us", my mom replied, shaking the long fork that she was holding at him. "You don't understand", my father loudly retorted, "I have to go with them. I should be at the Town Hall, it's safer for me, for us, if I go with them. Look, if something happens I'll be on the side of those throwing the stones not the ones getting them in the head."

Now that was smart, I thought, but it was a short-lived thought. The Marsa Mechanical workers were already passing my house, so my father jumped to his feet, took his coat and vanished.

I tried to run after him, but my mom's eyes stopped me short. I never saw that kind of look on her face and, shocked as I was, I decided to stay and comfort her. It turned out to my advantage in the end anyway. I got to finish my father's ribs too. With sour cabbage they were delicious. And that year's cabbage was especially good. We made it as always, about 200kg in a huge plastic barrel and, during the long months of winter it was present, in one form or another, every day on our table. But we couldn't finish it all so on special occasions we used to give some pickled cabbages to our gypsy neighbors who were always happy to receive them.

After eating my father's ribs I didn't leave mom for the TV. Together we continued to fry new ribs and put them in the big jars. They were salty and smelled good. A few months later, when completely covered in opaque white lard, every once in a while I would take one out with a fork, and eat it with white bread and onion. The truth was that I preferred to eat the ribs with fresh tomatoes, but when the tomato season started the ribs were already gone. My auntie's house in Brasov was where I had had ribs with fresh tomatoes in the middle of summer. My aunt had no children, so their pig was always too much for them, and that was why it always lasted so long.

Felicia, my sister came to call us upstairs to watch the Revolution together.

"'We' took over the TV station. The revolutionaries are speaking on TV, you have to hurry", she said hurrying herself with pickles and a super sized fried sausage. That 'we' that she used was the same one used when supporting the Romanian national team in soccer games. 'We' against the 'others', but on that particular occasion I didn't know who the 'others' were. I only knew Ceaușescu, and we were all against him.

My sister always ate pickles, and, when we had them, sausages. We grew up together but I cannot remember her ever eating soup. Or staying at the table until everyone had finished. Maybe that was the reason she was so small, so thin. Too many pickles, and to hell with everything else! Even now that she has turned 33, I don't think she is a gram over 40 kilos.

Before following her upstairs with a snack and a hot cocoa for myself, we had to help mother put the jars in the cool room. This room was adjacent to the kitchen, built so the sunshine never touched its walls. Its floor was non insulated concrete and it had two small and always open windows - one at floor level, and the other one under the ceiling - so even on a hot summer day the temperature inside never climbed above 9 degrees centigrade.

The next day was the day we had to melt the pig's fat into lard and pour it over the ribs, covering them, to keep them edible until summer. I had heard that some people kept their fried meat in oil, but my mother never veered from the traditional way. First of all the sunflower oil that was sold in Romania at the time had a rancid taste, and secondly because the dishes cooked with oil, and not with the traditional lard, were nothing like my mom's food.

As we settled down in front of the TV, our backs to the terracotta stove and the door, Ceaușescu was already being captured with his wife. They were ditched by their pilot who told them he had run out of gas, so they tried, farsically, to highjack a car to flee in. They promised the driver money, but they were turned in and brought to a military camp in Tragoviste, the former capital of Walachia, the very place from where our kings (including Vlad, the Impaler) had ruled from.

But we didn't know all that. We, like all Romanians, and the entire world that existed beyond our borders which was probably watching us, did not know that. But the people on the TV screen, the archangels of freedom, who proclaimed first the end of Ceauşescu and only later, under pressure from the revolutionary mob, the end of communist rule in Romania, knew. They were already preparing the Ceauşescus' slaughter. The summary trial. The execution.

But they said nothing about their plans. Nor anything about their already having taken control of the country. Instead they called on the people to come out of their homes and onto the streets, to defend the Revolution.

"Come and defend the TV station", they urged on air. And my mother's hands turned whiter and whiter as she clung to her armchair with an ever-tightening grip.

She didn't voice it but I could see she was worried about father, being caught now in a similar turmoil. What if he had to "defend the revolution"? What if he was shot and killed? Now the TV, not Radio Free Europe was talking about thousands and thousands of deaths, about people murdered, cremated and dumped in sewage drains.

"Come and help me with the smoke", my mom said, and I felt that she was trying to do something, anything, other than just sitting there, worried about my father, about us, about the Revolution.

"What do you think will happen?" I asked, and she responded, blurting out the words:

"We will have food".

"What do you mean, we will have food?" My question came because all I could think of were the sausages being smoked in OUR smokehouse, the jambon still in salt, the two huge pig-long pieces of fatback in salt, in OUR basement too.

"Remember when we went on that trip to Hungary?" asked my mother like she was dreaming with her eyes wide open. "There was plenty of food. Remember the supermarket with plenty of meats and cheese and bread and nobody waited in long lines to buy anything. The people didn't look desperate like shoppers do here."

"But, mom, Hungary was a communist country, back then."

"I know, but I heard that in Germany stores are even bigger, and better supplied than in Hungary."

Her argument was undefeatable so I put my handmade ski hat on to go outside. I usually did not bother with a coat, but I always took a hat, when going outside. Gloves, too, sometimes. When door handles drop in temperature 20 below zero, I had better wear gloves before touching them. Otherwise, my hands would stick to them, which is an interesting sight to see, but not to experience.

Anyway, it wasn't that cold on that 22nd of December, so I decided to go with just my hat. My mom followed me and I really did not understand why. It was my job to light the fire, not hers, so I assumed she didn't really trust my way of doing it or my ability.

The fire in the bucket was still going, under layers of willow sawdust, but it desperately needed more wood chips. Carefully I started to remove the burned and unburned sawdust to uncover the amber coals. I covered them with big chunks of dry willow and started to blow my lungs out to start a new fire. Soon I was done. But just as I was about to cover that new fire in wooden chips and willow sawdust, my mom threw something in the flames.

I understood what when I saw it opening and a very young and thin version of my father started to burn. She was burning their Communist Party ID cards, two small cranberry red booklets containing their names and pictures and a few stamps.

"It's getting hot in here, you better cover the fire", she stated dreamily. I obeyed, thinking how long it would take for my father's picture to burn, how that smoke would affect the sausages hanging above and why it was necessary for her to burn those IDs. It was impossible to hide their membership in the Communist Party, if that was what she was trying to do. Everybody we knew were communists. Both of my grandmothers were not, but my grandfather, the only one I knew, was a communist. Not a proud one. He was forced to hand over his horse to the communist government in the early '60s, but he was red.

Soon, the smoke was thick enough for us to leave. I wanted to go upstairs to watch more television. I was 14 and television hungry. We had only two hours of mostly news about Ceaușescu and the countries he had visited, and I wanted more television.

In the summer of 1989, I was in Lodroman, the village where my maternal grandmother used to live and watched three American movies. One was a Vietnam war movie, the other one was a police movie and the last one a comedy. I had paid the owner of the VCR player 60 lei for me and my sister and that was the first time I had seen a color television. I sat for nearly 5 hours on the floor, in a room covered with teenagers, all of them paying all their savings to watch those movies, and I wished communism would end so that we could buy our own color TV set and VCR player. I guess freedom for me back in 1989 was nothing more and nothing less.

Two years on, in 1991 I was watching the same Opera TV set and I still did not have a VCR player. Only in the summer of 1992 did we have the money to buy a secondhand German-made Blaupunkt color TV set and a secondhand Japanese Akai VCR player. It was a big event, not only for us, but for all our neighbors, too, who gathered at our house. We all watched, in a cramped room, the same Vietnam war movie that I had seen in 1989, in the summertime, and my only thought was how stupid I was to believe that freedom was watching lots of TV and owning home entertainment systems. I could not help but observe how my happy-to-be-there neighbors envied us for having that color TV set, even if it was an old one which came in a retro wooden box, probably one that some very fat Germans full of beer and hot dogs, threw out on New Year's Day, along with an over-sized VCR player, made in 1983 by Akai, a maker that was better known in Romania than in Japan.

But of course back on December 22nd, 1989, I was still a child. One that was very difficult to entertain. I had read all of my fathers 1000 or so books and the insignificant tiny town library had nothing I was interested in reading. Reading was my life but in my countryside I had already read all I could get my hands on. I even read the Bible that very year, mainly because it was the only book I hadn't read on our bookshelves...And, to my surprise, I found it to be a good book!

Maybe that was the reason I was desperate to watch TV, to watch American movies...Our communist society urged us to be secular, and the capitalist era that started in 1989 made that a priority too. So, soon I had my share of my long dreamed of American entertainment and in my first year of "freedom" I proudly kept records of all the American movies I managed to watch. And I didn't stop until I had more than 1000 entries in that scrapbook and considered myself the most pathetic idiot of the free world. Freedom was more than eating popcorn and watching Hollywood movies, that's for sure.

But, back on that 22nd of December, 1989, my sister was still watching the TV rejoicing at her new freedom but somehow worried. It was already getting dark and shooting had started around all the Revolution hot spots, the TV station and the Central Committee building. Later that night our new leader, self-elected with the memorable expression "with your permission I'll sign my name as the last on this list" spoken the moment he wrote his name ABOVE everyone else's, Ion Iliescu, was delivering a speech from the very balcony Ceaușescu last spoke to us, and shooting began, but nobody shot at him, they all shot at the buildings around the square. The National Museum of Art was devastated, dozens of paintings forever lost, the University Library was set on fire, thousands and thousands of precious books and documents forever lost, some homes around the square were reduced to ashes along with the people inhabiting them. Their memories were lost forever. Who were they?

But we didn't miss any of Iliescu's speech and we came to love him the way we used to love Ceaușescu. He looked invincible. Speaking from that balcony while everybody was shooting around. Surely the terrorists were lousy shooters.

Nobody in that lighted balcony got killed, but people didn't notice the absurdity of it. The evidence. All they wanted to see was a new leader to believe in, a new leader to follow.

And Romanians followed him. In the May elections held in 1989 Iliescu won the same way the late Saddam Hussein won in Iraq when he was still alive and dictator, but again I was very young and I didn't know all that. That part of history hadn't happened yet, we still had time to change it and prevent it, but we did nothing at all. I sat myself down beside my sister, tried another sip of the now very cold cocoa, and watched the TV like in a trance.

Actually it was captivating. It was like a good movie, a kind of thriller being played and made at the same time. The terrorists (it was made clear by Iliescu that all those shooting their guns were terrorists hired by Ceauşescu to help him get back in power) were ruthless and they were attacking the squares where Ion Iliescu and Petre Roman, a nice guy with no neck wearing a sweater, were.

God, I hated the terrorists.

Night fell and my father came back from work. He came back from the city hall where the revolution was in full swing. And because he was a good storyteller he wanted to tell us that particular story in a much better environment, so my mom came up with a crazy idea and we all started to prepare my father's set. The idea was to bring a dining table up to the room my sister and I shared and dine together while we watched the televised revolution and listen to my father's story. So we started by folding up my bed, which transformed into a couch, we took the armchairs into the next room and brought from downstairs a dining table and chairs. My mom went into the closet and pulled out the most expensive embroidered white tablecloth we had and glasses followed, then the porcelain and it looked like a party, only that this party was held in front of a TV set and in an unlikely place, the kids' room.

Now, when you picture this kids' room, think of bookshelves holding half of my father's books, two very decent beds draped in cobalt blue covers, one heavy wardrobe that would make proud any granny in Old England, the TV stand, full of books under the TV set, and a blood red carpet, so the room didn't look like a kids' room looks in American movies. Still I was shocked. It was my room and all the adults in my house had gathered there to watch the televised revolution AND eat, another unlikely event.

It was the end of communism and the beginning of freedom, my father told us, so why not, we had to somehow acknowledge that freedom, that we had somehow gotten, and that party was just a way to express it, I thought.

Soon white bread, pickles, meats and zacusca were on the table and my mother promised us more homemade delicacies were awaiting us the following day. Nobody stood with their backs to the TV set, and for the first hour we just watched in silence.

"You know, the mayor was literally sent home to wash dishes by the Marsa Mechanical workers". The mayor at the time was a woman. Never before and never again since. She wasn't elected mayor but selected by the communist government. All nearby cities had women as mayors and all of them were sent home by the angry people "to cook for their husbands and wash dishes". It all went off "with no violence". That was the slogan the crowds in Bucharest chanted while they were being shot at by the hidden terrorists. Although, not all of them went down without a fight. My father lowered his voice when he spoke of how the mayor of Cisnadie was stripped of her clothes and paraded naked to her house by the town's "revolutionaries", and I was sure he didn't like it.

"You should have seen them, lots of people happy and celebrating, but even more drunk". "They destroyed everything in the Town Hall", my father went on. Lucky for us, the town's self-proclaimed Revolution leader was Mr. Tatu, my best friend's father. As a veterinary doctor he was a guarantee of honesty and good conduct.

"All my life I dreamed about this moment", he said when he entered the Town Hall's mayoral office, and he recalled the time his father, a priest, was imprisoned many years by the communists for just being a priest and how he, his son, was expelled from medical school before graduating, how he was denied the right to a higher education. How he had struggled to become a veterinarian, in a place where people had no pets but only animals that served them. Cows and horses to be helped birthing, pigs to be castrated so that their meat would taste good, and chickens to be vaccinated. In Avrig nobody bothered to name their cats and dogs. They were just servants, cats to chase away mice, dogs to chase away thieves. Nobody cared if they died. They could be replaced immediately, and for free, so nothing to occupy a vet.

Mr. Tatu was to become the first MP from Avrig to serve in Parliament from 1990 to 1992. We saw him on the TV a few months later, and we were proud. The people in that first parliament tried to build a democratic regime without knowing what a democratic regime is, they had no more idea what a democracy is than we did, sitting at that table, on the evening of December 22nd, 1989. Entertainment, food, that was what a democratic regime meant to all Romanians, sober or otherwise. After pouring himself a glass of red wine, which, being homemade in late autumn, smelled fruity and fresh, my father continued his story.

"They completely destroyed the bookstore", he announced looking us in our shocked eyes:

"And the library too".

Now that was more than unsettling, it was really bad news. The bookstore was the store I loved more than any other. Next door to my auntie Anişoara's house, it displayed not only books that I loved to buy but also stationery and toys. It was always crowded and would have been especially crowded this time of year. The reason was simple: that bookstore, destroyed and, as I learned later, looted by the revolutionaries, was the only spot my folks could buy me a Christmas present.

Felicia started to cry. She got it too. No Christmas presents this year. She didn't believe in Father Christmas anymore. I had told her a couple of years earlier that our parents were the real

Santa Claus, but still, she was 13 years old and was looking forward to that Christmas more than anything else.

I knew that my father would always wait until the very last moment to buy Christmas presents for us. He always did. He didn't like to rush things and he was also afraid that we would find the presents hidden in the house before Christmas and that was unacceptable. Father Christmas had to come late at night on Christmas Eve, sometimes impersonated by one of my father's friends, or, simply by putting the presents under the Christmas tree when nobody was around.

"Why did those morons do something so barbarous?" my sister asked sobbing while collapsing on her bed. She sat there crying and later listening to us all evening until she fell into a deep sleep. Revolutions are too difficult for little girls to grasp.

"They wanted to burn all the books about Ceauşescu. And all the books with pictures of Ceauşescu", my father explained. "And they did. There was a huge fire in the middle of the street, and people got caught up in the heat of the moment. They started burning everything that they were vandalizing".

I didn't know then, and neither did my family, that earlier that day Ceauşescu's dogs, two black Labradors presented to him by Queen Elisabeth and Sir David Steele were clubbed to death by revolutionaries who obviously got caught up in the heat of the moment. How else can those who did the clubbing explain why they did it? I'm sure it was more gruesome than just burning innocent books, than just smashing windows with stones. But Revolutions are bloody and, as I was familiar with the details of the French Revolution, I expected violence. But violence against Ceauşescu-lovers, not against books or dogs.

The heat of the moment? I was thinking about that explanation when I realized that they must have burned the school books too. They all had Ceauşescu's picture on the first page, just behind the cover and, it was the beginning of our freedom, of democracy, so why not? Secretly I wished my father had looted a "Romanian language" textbook for me. Mine was so old and falling to bits. I was easily the 6th or 7th owner.

In those days we had to get our textbooks from the motherland. But our communist state was poor, Ceauşescu was trying to pay off all our foreign debt and there was less and less money for us, the kids. Therefore, on the last day of the school year we had to give all our textbooks back to our principal. The teachers would mend them, glue them where necessary, and decide what textbooks could be re-used. Interestingly enough, it seemed that their standards dropped every year. Anyway, when done they would order only the bare minimum of new books, and that was always too few...It was hard for me to remember the last time I got a new book. Was it when I was in first grade? Or the second? It didn't matter. All that mattered was that the revolutionaries had burned the textbooks too. The textbooks that they never bought for their kids.

"I won't buy you a new textbook", my father once said. "You can use the one that you got from school. If you can read it, if it's not missing any of its pages, then it serves its purpose", he ruled. Sure they did. My old and decrepit textbooks were there for me when I became fifth in my class. Actually, when I became fifth, I did not want to rise any higher but neither did I want to fall lower. Behind me trailed the rest of my class, the other 39 students. But what purpose had burning those textbooks served? Why were they burned? Because they had a picture of Ceauşescu in them or because the workers that had set them alight wanted to take revenge on the school they did not love so much? The only place that they did not destroy was the local pub. The pub did nothing wrong to them, maybe, and despite what their wives thought, they spared it, went in and ordered drinks, for which they paid. Poor workers, pity their kids and the burned school books. I was too young at the time to have known, but my second guess was right. A few months later in Bucharest coal miners started beating to death or just beating, or just clubbing, or just chasing anybody who looked intellectual.

"We work, we don't think" was the slogan that united them against those wearing beards or glasses. They were called to defend the new power, to defend Ion Iliescu and Petre Roman, against the anti-communist parties that organized demonstrations to push for a different change. A change that would exclude ex-communists from public life for at least eight years.

But I was too young. So young that I hated Silviu Brucan, a smart ass Romanian Jew who said that "Romanians are many and stupid" when he predicted that the real change was to come only after 2009, twenty years on. But a few years on all I wanted to be was like Brucan. His books were intelligent, he had arguments, he was always telling the truth. To be Romania's new Brucan. What a beautiful dream! But back in 1989 I was disgusted. My father was disgusted, too, because he didn't know that Brucan said in one of his books that the Revolution turned Romania into a train without a driver. And when nobody knew where the train's engine was, Iliescu and his team (Brucan included) climbed on and took the controls. My father would have agreed with that.

But I was too young to know that. And my father was too naive in his expectations to have known that. He, like all Romanians who had partied in front of their TV sets or threw away their lives on the streets of Bucharest and Sibiu, had naive expectations of the power change. Now that Ceaușescu had fled and the Revolution had happened, a democratic regime would follow, not another dictatorship, the stores would be filled with goods, everybody would be well-dressed, like in those Nekerman catalogues from West Germany we sometimes had a chance to see.

The new power, the devil who went by the name of Iliescu, however, had other plans.

"Nicolae Ceaușescu tarnished the noble ideals of Socialism", Iliescu said earlier that day on TV, hoping he would become a Gorbachev. Because he couldn't be a Havel. He had to be a Gorbachev. Brucan had been in Moscow earlier that year, not that we, the people, were aware of that, getting orders to organise the Ceaușescus' fall. Glasnost and Perestroika were being implemented in the USSR and it had to happen in Romania too. But Ceaușescu was old, he was stubborn, he was a Stalinist.

Ceaușescu had to be replaced by Iliescu, and that was why Iliescu was called on, after the Revolution had started, from his office as head of a publishing house, to take control. And he did take control. He signed, as head of that publishing house, documents relating to the capture and trial of the two Ceaușescus. Strange that nobody questioned who he was, strange that they let him appoint General Militaru as the Army Chief.

My father was just finishing his story about the vandalism in our tiny town, and my mom was just finishing her meal. I was eating fresh white bread and was trying to decide if it would be better to put some pate on it or not.

And so General Militaru was introduced. He looked old and he looked tall. He was ugly, without doubt, but he promised to help the Revolution. The Army was on our side, and as its new chief of staff he made sure it stayed with us, with the people, with the Revolution. We did not know that General Militaru (his name in Romanian means the military man) was a soviet agent, but Iliescu did. He was his man, and that man was there for a job, but nobody watching TV or dying on the streets was aware of that.

He was replacing, the story went, General Vasile Milea.

"Who?" I asked my father, and he said that General Milea was the one who saluted Ceaușescu during the military parade every August 23rd, the day of our communist motherfuckinland. And I vaguely remembered a rather fat uniform, saluting with pride, the dictatorial couple.

"General Vasile Milea was a hero" was the story that was told by the blaring black and white Opera TV set, and he was killed by forces loyal to Ceaușescu. That was the story and that was the reason why the new power named several long boulevards after him, one of them in Sibiu. But he wasn't killed. He shot himself, aiming for the heart, but he missed. He killed himself for not being able to stop the Revolution. He died of blood loss in his office, the very one from which the armed forces were ordered against defenseless civilians during the events of the previous days. That was the official verdict of a criminal investigation into his death. The conclusion was reached in 2005, long after all of us had gotten used to his name, and gotten used to taking buses from General Vasile Milea Boulevard to the train station.

"I need you two to help me with the pots for the lard. I will start making it first thing in the morning, but the pots are too heavy and I need you to set them on the stove". My mom was always practical. There was a Revolution happening, but so was the lard making, and she could not miss the chance to do it right. That lard was the grease that our health depended on in 1990, it made up a good part of the ingredients of our soap, it kept our pig ribs safe from mold, and so on.

"Let's wash those pots, first of all", my father said.

"I'm sure they're dusty".

We entered the basement, where those two 50 liter pots were waiting for us. We used them to make lard, various kinds of jam, the zacusca and the tomato juice I loved to drink after school. But they were stored in the basement most of the time, which meant we had to wash them before using them, every time. We washed them outside, with hot water fetched from the kitchen, near the place where we slaughtered the pig. Despite the fact that we had cleaned the spot afterwards, the now frozen dirt was still coal black from the straw fire that had burned off the pig's hair and dirt.

Once washed we went inside the kitchen and put one pot on the hub and the other on the stove. We had a hub that we used mainly in summer and a stove that we used, for the extra heat, in winter. Between them was the water tap which we used to put some water in both of those huge pots. If we were cannibals those pots would have easily accommodated some people for boiling, but we weren't. My mom would put the pig's fat and all the fatty parts of the pig in them, first thing the following morning, and boil them until all the fat dissolved and, before all the water was gone, she would turn off the fire under the pots and add salt. Then she would put the hot lard in the jars that held the fried ribs and the remaining lard into small jars that she would use for cooking. Vegetable oil was only used in our house when fasting, before Christmas and before Easter and every Wednesday and Friday throughout the year. We were supposed to be fasting and not eat meat, fish, milk, eggs or anything made from them. Lard was from our pig and she could not cook with it on those days.

When I got back upstairs, the lights were off, but the TV was still blaring out light and sound. My sister was sleeping and my mom had cleared the table of food. My father's glass of wine and a half full carafe were waiting. From the TV I soon learned that people in Bucharest had been called on to stay in the streets to defend the revolution. That the so-called terrorists were "shooting from all sides" and that the TV station was under heavy attack. "Come and defend the TV station", Iliescu or one of his team encouraged the citizens and those fearing a Ceauşescu comeback stayed on the streets. "Shoot on sight", was the televised message to all the soldiers who were fighting for the revolution.

I got into my bed which was not more than a couch and closed my eyes.

"What if the people going to defend the TV station are mistaken for terrorists?" my father asked and the sanity of his question occupied my thoughts until I was dreaming. What bothers me still today is the fact that I can remember that day so clearly, without being able to remember my dream. Perhaps that dream was not so important, but I now think it was. Sometimes I have premonitions in my dreams. That massacre took place while I was still dreaming.

3. DECEMBER 23RD

The fact is that Iliescu had to get a stronger grip on power. The fact is that General Militaru was his man. The fact is that the crowd started to doubt his leadership after he morphed into a Gorbachov and not into a Havel. The fact is that Romanians had to unite against Ceaușescu. Around the new leadership. The fact is that the same Romanians did not know that Ceaușescu had been caught and was waiting for a summary trial, nor the fact that the plan was to execute the two of them anyway. Maybe I wasn't the only one familiar with the French Revolution, maybe I wasn't the only one who thought a Revolution must be bloody for Ceaușescu-lovers. For certain, someone was aware of that when he hit the panic button: there were no Ceaușescu-lovers to fight. There were no Ceaușescu-lovers for the people to unite against, no pigs to be sacrificed for the greater good.

So, while I was turning in my sleep, dreaming the dream that I cannot remember, the Air Force Chief of Staff, General Iosif

Rus, was hanging up his military phone after he had barked his orders.

He did what he had to do, not knowing the bigger picture, perhaps, and went to sleep, too, satisfied with the way power had changed hands. Those who got his orders were already awake. They were no younger than 18 and no older than 19. They were only kids. Some of them, from the countryside, had never seen running water from taps, nor trains, nor helicopters before being enlisted in the military.

They were sleepy. They had been listening to the Revolution on the radio so long. I didn't know because I hadn't been listening to the national radio station, but there had been a revolution there too. All hopes of freedom and all the anger directed at Ceauşescu invaded the Romanian airwaves for those that did not have a TV set, not so few in those days, especially in the countryside. But everyone had a radio, and some soldiers had radios too.

"I reckon when this Revolution is over, we'll all get to go home sooner" someone said with hope, in the dark, after the light was turned off at 9 pm in their stinking dormitory. The thought, spoken out loud, had come from the area of the room that hosted those with the longest AMR in their unit (in Romanian AMR stands for 'Au Mai Rămas xxx Zile' or 'There are xxx days left') so everybody started to laugh. New draftees were called ducklings and everyone loved to pick on them. But, when a new batch of draftees entered the unit, the previous batch would be called "veterans" and they would do to the new ducklings all the shit they had endured during their first six months, sometimes more.

The next group of ducklings was only weeks away. That meant that a third of the soldiers in that dorm were weeks away from their "liberation day". The current ducklings had another year on their AMR and that was why it was so funny. The one with the radio turned it down and soon they were all asleep. The air was heavy. On that day they had to wash their uniforms and, because the glorious Romanian Army gave them only one each, the next day they had to wear them, wet or not.

In the Romania of 1989, that military unit had no clothes dryers, not even ironing facilities. So they did as all soldiers do in that kind of situation: they laid the wet clothes neatly on their mattresses, covered them with their blankets and slept on them, covering themselves with the remaining two sheets. It wasn't comfortable, but the woollen blankets would suck out almost all the water from their uniforms and the next day these uniforms would look like they had been freshly ironed. Albeit, still wet. In any case, the uniforms would be in better shape than if hung up to dry in that room, and in the morning, when they awoke, at least their uniforms would be there. Sometimes, perhaps often, low-lifes would steal uniforms in better shape than their own because the motherfuckingland was too poor to give them new uniforms just like it was too poor to give us new textbooks.

Then again, in those days everybody used to steal. When the shops were empty, and stomachs empty, too, the country's economy changed into a barter economy. People would steal products from the companies they were working for and trade those products for others, until they managed to trade something for food. The military was no different. Even the words used to describe it changed. Nobody used the word "steal" anymore. "Steal" was negative. So they used "complete" instead. They were "completing" their needs, and having your wet uniform under your butt was the same as keeping it safe, out of reach of any "completing" that was going on at night.

Usually the uniforms were almost dry at 6 in the morning, and they were perfect after breakfast, but that wasn't to be the case that particular day. The alarm sounded at 3:00am when they had almost another three hours of welcomed sleep ahead of them. Swear words, curses, a corporal hitting crying ducklings. The air was damper than usual. Wet socks on skeletal feet, wet underwear on, wet shirt on, a dry sweater, the uniform, also still wet, dry boots, a dry winter coat, a dry winter hat, all went on. Gloves on hands and they were running. Everybody took an AKM on their way out and the frost fiercely attacked their knees, and it was like the marrow was being sucked out of their bones and their bones were like those in "racituri", the pig gelatin they had with black pepper every January 1st.

The 83 kids dressed in army uniforms were lined up in the cold night and read the mission. Terrorists were going to attack the International Airport, the only International Airport that Romania had. Ceauşescu's plane, that fabulous 707 that copied the American Air Force One, was there on the tarmac, and Ceauşescu planned to attack the airport, get on it and flee Romania with all the people's money. So they had to fight back, they had to protect the airport.

I was still sleeping when they got in the three military trucks that their unit was able to somehow scrape. Fuel was scarce that day, and filling the fuel tanks with diesel had required emptying the fuel tanks of all cars and trucks parked there. Ceauşescu's plane. Cold and freezing, everyone of them dreamed they would have a chance to get on it soon. But not one of them did.

I was asleep at 5 in the morning and dreaming my impossible-to-remember dream. Did I fly in Ceauşescu's plane in my dream? I don't know. I was afraid of flying. My father called planes "flying coffins". But six years later, when I flew for the first time in my life, I flew in that plane.

Back in 1996, I was working as a journalist to pay for my studies in journalism. My father had been dead more than a year when I was sent abroad to the Former Yugoslav Republic of Macedonia to write about Meleşcanu's visit there. Meleşcanu was the head of the Ministry of Foreign Affairs, a hotshot, married to a newscaster. A good communist.

And the Macedonians wanted to kill me.

The train I boarded in Sofia, Bulgaria, emptied in Nish. It stopped there for several hours before starting to move again towards Macedonia. It was my first time abroad, but it wasn't exciting. Maybe because I looked too young. I was 20 but I didn't even look 19. And I was traveling with an American soldier.

"US Army?"

"Yes."

"In the business of slaughtering people?"

"No, in the one of saving them!"

"So you save the real slaughterers?"

"If I get lucky I get to save their victims too".

He was a M.A.S.H. and had spent his leave in Istanbul and was heading back to his unit in Skopje. He was looking to buy some food but there wasn't any. Yugoslavia was a country – or I should say still a country – devastated by ethnic war. I offered him a couple of sandwiches I was carrying with me.

"Try these. They're made with Sibiu Salami, the best salami in the whole world" I said, and he liked them. We talked. M.A.S.H was being aired in Romania at the time and he saw the word on the TV program guide in the paper I was carrying and he thought it was funny. He was the first American I ever met and he was a good talker. But we stopped at the border and armed guards entered our compartment. They searched him, but not like they searched me. My bag flew open and I was embarrassed. My underwear was everywhere and I felt like I had lost my dignity, and they were asking me for money.

500 Deutschemarks, and I didn't want to give it to them and they pulled me out of the train, pushing me with their guns until inside the train station's office. Some uniforms were playing poker. A wooden table, lots of money. Money that I recognized and money that I didn't. Bottles with spirits. Serbian slivovitz. Or Macedonian. Or whatever. They were drinking straight from those bottles. And there were guns too. On the same table. The one who looked like the boss wrote "500DM" on a piece of newspaper. They were quite organized, I thought, asking for the same price. With those guns on the table he could have easily asked for double that. But I didn't pay so, with a black, over-sized handgun in his hand he said something to me. But I heard nothing. It was the second time I had been so close to a gun. The first time was during the Revolution and that gun was on a table, too, beside a bottle of brandy. I was lightheaded, and I started to think whether what I was feeling was indeed fear.

They could kill me on the spot and nobody would know I had been on that train. That was what was going through my head when I started to lie. I told them in English I was a journalist, going to Skopje to interview their president, a guy called Gligorov. It seemed that they did not understand a word so I tried to repeat that Gligorov word, over and over again. I wasn't there for Gligorov, I was there for Meleşcanu, but they didn't know who the fuck Meleşcanu was, nor did they care.

The boss stood up and he didn't look happy, he showed me the gun and suddenly a door opened and a young female officer entered and asked me in English for a Press ID, and I handed mine to her. Suddenly she was half screaming at them and the boss barked some order and a soldier took me by the arm and rushed me outside. I thought they were going to shoot me but then I saw the train and it was moving. First slowly and then faster, and the soldier was half carrying me towards it and I climbed in half disembodied. I had managed to catch a hold of the last handle of the last door. An unlikely scene, because it was night on the border between Yugoslavia, still a country back in 1996, and FYROM, something pretending to be a country but which at the time was not.

The shocked M.A.S.H was packing my bag. The incident brought us together in that train and that was the only incident on the way to our destination. We said our goodbyes. We were young, with hopes of a bright future. But so were the soldiers from Campina, when they boarded those three trucks six years earlier.

We did not know that September 11 would come, and in 1989 the soldiers from Campina knew even less. We didn't know that the US would fight another three wars over the following years, that his countrymen would bomb the shit out of Serbia beyond the border we had just crossed.

The short story is that I had heard that Meleşcanu had come in a 707, Ceauşescu's plane, to open the Romanian embassy there. Romania was still a poor country in 1996 and its kids still used decrepit textbooks in school, but we were spending the pennies we had on our diplomatic shit. And we were so proud of our shit.

"Excellency, you should see the residence of our ambassador. He lives better than any other European ambassador here", said one of Meleşcanu's trusted men, very proud of himself.

Anyway, I told the folks in the Embassy my story and they arranged for me to fly back to Bucharest in the same plane, but only after they accused me of trying to ruin the friendship between the two countries with absurd claims and that everything I had said was in order to get a free ride back on the 707. It was a "convenient claim", as the moron in the embassy had put it.

So we went to the airport. A rather small one. Smaller than the central train station built by some Japanese companies after the earthquake that flattened Macedonia in the 70's. Romania had built some flats there, too, after the same earthquake, and I could pick them out quite easily. They were the ugliest in Skopje. Not that they were any uglier than the flats back home.

We got on that plane and it looked nice, it had a saloon, and furniture, but it was no Air Force One, or at least not what we see in American movies. I sat in the back beside a Romanian pilot I had met in Skopje, in that hotel where I could not flush my toilet and nobody cared to clean my room. He, too, was offered a bottle to pour tap water in the toilet after he took a dump. And we were going up and down and up and down and left and then right. And so it went on and on.

"Not a bad landing for a beginner", said my pilot friend, and after we landed everyone was patting Meleşcanu on the back:

"Well done, Mr. Minister".

"That was the smoothest landing I ever experienced, your Excellency".

Before 1989 all we had was Ceauşescu, but it was 1996 and we were free. People still "completed", when they could, everything they wanted from our motherfuckingland, and Meleşcanu wanted to land a 707. Ceauşescu's 707...Others wanted more. That was the reason why those 83 kids from Campina had to die quickly, like my pig. Big shots were waiting in line for benefits.

45

Back in those trucks it was bloody cold. There were twenty soldiers in each one, seated face to face on the two benches in the back of the trucks. You know, you've seen that scene hundreds of times in American movies. But the soldiers in the three trucks did not look like those American hotshots. First of all they were all thin. Secondly, they were just kids. Thirdly, they were scared and tired.

It was so bloody cold. The cold that they welcomed at home when smoking sausages. Actually those sausages were on everyone's mind. In a couple of days, on Christmas Day, their moms would come to visit and they would bring fresh sausages. And white bread. And they would sit down on a bench and wolf if all down while their mothers cried. They would cry at the sight of their babies so thin, so malnourished, so much more men than before they left home.

Only the luckiest would get 24 hours leave, but with the shooting in Bucharest it was pointless believing you had such luck. A couple of soldiers opened their packs of biscuits and started to eat them with cheese. Another thing one does not, cannot, see in American movies. In those movies soldiers eat chocolate and square meals. The 83 from Campina got no chocolate when they got in their trucks, only a pack of army biscuits, made without any butter or vegetable oil and so hard they had to keep them in their mouths for a long time before taking a bite. Then there were the three shapeless pieces of cheese, expired maybe years before that December night in 1989...They had their own water in their canteens, tap water, the coldest tap water in Romania, the very same that washed their uniforms the night before.

They were too young and, as I already said, much like myself, unaware that those biscuits with cheese were about to become their last supper. They sat close to each other to catch each other's body heat, closing their eyes, some of them going back to sleep.

"You can say you are a soldier only when you are able to sleep while standing and walking", my father used to tell me, proud indeed that he had served. Years later, I am proud I didn't.

I became a man without serving in the Army, but it happened that way only because of the revolution. Otherwise, I would have had to serve for probably one year in the military. Military training for a couple of months and then, for the rest of the term, working in agriculture, or construction, as was customary those days.

But I didn't serve because, and it sounds so egotistical, those 83 big children from Campina, and others like them were about to die for me, for us, for nothing.

Death was waiting. Impatiently. The trucks stopped at a checkpoint. It was the Airport security's first checkpoint. As with all other checkpoints they were let through. A few hundred meters closer to the airport and the trucks had to stop again. Another checkpoint. This time a uniform that survivors would know later as lieutenant-major Ionescu, got in the first truck to show them the way, he claimed. But his orders were to wait there, which he couldn't anymore. It was cold, so cold, and he wanted to get out of the cold, to have a smoke. So the uniform got in and with a smelly burst the trucks were on the move again and someone dropped his canteen and water was spilling all over and suddenly there was more blood spilling than water, faces missing, the terrible sound of bullets hitting the truck and the even more terrible sound of bullets biting through winter coats, finally dry uniforms...and flesh. 22 soldiers were killed in seconds. Engines died too. Somewhere in the distance machine guns were rattling at them.

Even if you have slaughtered a pig or you watched a pig being slaughtered for you, you still cannot imagine the fresh human blood flowing in that truck. With the pig things are controlled, the blood is collected in a bucket, and the meat, when the pig is opened with a knife, looks more like the meat you see at a butcher's: it doesn't bleed.

But not human flesh. I know that because I had to listen many times to Uncle Gheorghe and his war stories. Uncle Gheorghe was my grandmother's brother-in-law and in WWII he came home only because he was a better killer. Better than those seven Russians and five Germans that he killed with his knife and bare hands.

Uncle Vasile, my grandmother's brother, was not as tough. As a baker he loved his bread and loved the people who ate it, so he was killed in WWI, by French troops, and he definitely did not fight back. He died like a lamb, my grandmother used to say. She couldn't use the word "pig", despite the fact that those Frenchmen who got her brother saw in him not the baker whose bread they would have loved to eat, but a pig wearing an Austrian uniform.

"With pigs it's easy", Uncle Gheorghe used to say, "but people die very hard". "What you see in the movies (and he was referring to the Soviet movies about WWII) is nothing but lies". "People are not like pigs. You can sometimes put your knife a dozen times into a body and that body will still fight back" he used to warn us, the kids sitting around him. Then he would show us his wounds, his knife wounds, and he would point out which ones he got from Germans and which from Russians, only he could tell them apart.

Years later, Uncle Gheorghe died, but when he did he was still amazed at the news that 22 soldiers were killed almost instantly in those trucks.

"Surely they were hit by dozens of bullets each" he said and he cried. For him that was not the definition of friendly fire, but the definition of a well-organized firing squad. "They were like Ilie", and Ilie, his son, came back in one piece from his army time, married and had a daughter, unlike those 22 killed suddenly, sprayed with bullets, after their trucks were cleared at the checkpoint.

That morning I woke up at six and got out of my bed quickly to go to the toilet downstairs. At exactly the same time the survivors got out of their trucks and took cover behind them or ran towards the forest.

"Don't shoot! Stop shooting!" the screams were heard in perfect Romanian. But they were being shot at from three different points in that ambush and if one started to shoot, the others followed suit.

"We surrender!"
"We surrender!"
"We surrender!"
"We surrender!"
"We surrender!"
"We surrender!"

But nobody cared. Those defending the airport had orders to kill. It was strange because the airport wasn't even closed. Taxis were coming and going, people were arriving for work in buses. A bus came into view minutes after those first 22 had already been slaughtered and it, too, entered the kill zone. The machine guns rattled and 8 civilians got killed in an instant, "how was that possible?" Uncle Gheorghe wandered again, questioning not the killing but their instant deaths. "People don't die like pigs. They need more time", he used to say to me, and he took his time. On his death bed he took his time, and it was painful for Aunt Parachiva to watch and for Ilie, too, just like it was painful for Uncle Gheorghe to watch those Germans and Russians dying and not being able to comfort them in a language they understood.

Twenty years and two months after that bus entered the kill zone, the survivors and the killers alike claim that the people in it were lucky. Twisted, isn't it? Of course, they had bad karma that day. They got up on time, they showed up to the bus station on time and despite there being a Revolution, the bus got there and picked them up, on time. Now that's bad karma. On the other hand, the bus driver wasn't killed and put the bus into reverse and drove as fast as he could, blood spilling from the closed doors, the cold wind rushing in through the shattered windows, until he and his bus were out of range.

He must have asked himself, "What the hell were the soldiers defending the airport thinking?". And they must have been thinking the same thing, too, because the surviving soldiers started to hear orders that made sense:

"Drop your weapons".

Now that was useless. They had dropped their weapons well before that, without having fired them.

"Stand up. Hands up".

Reluctantly, with fear mixed with hope, they did as they were told.

"Start walking towards the airport".

Which they did. 61 survivors and that Ionescu, the one uniform that had joined them on their deadly ride started to march, to follow the orders. They got closer. Closer. They could see the faces of their friends' killers. The killers could see that they were just a bunch of kids, thin and scared in Romanian Army uniforms. Unarmed. Not dangerous at all.

Ra,ta,ta,ta,ta,ta,ta...

The professional soldiers defending the airport opened fire again. And 17 were killed again, to Uncle's Gheorghe's disbelief, instantly. 12 others were wounded. They were the ones that confirmed my uncle's theory, they didn't die quickly. 11 of them pulled through.

Private Vasile Buta wanted to pull through, too, but his karma was particularly bad. His family name, Buta, is the Japanese for "pig", but he didn't know that. Yet. I hadn't that particular knowledge, either, despite the fact that 20 years after those events I was fluent in Japanese.

Private Buta was wounded in both legs. Paul Bustiuc, formerly Private Paul Bustiuc, was his friend. "They took us prisoners and they forbade us to help the wounded" he recalls in a hushed voice. "He could have lived. He might have lost a leg, or both, but not his life" he speaks to journalists, angry. And I was a journalist in 1996 because my father had died, too, and I needed money to stay in college in Bucharest.

Out of all the people slaughtered that day, private Buta died a pig's death. He was left to bleed "like a pig" recalls Paul, until his 5 liters of blood drained from his body, which, opened for the autopsy a few days later, looked cleaner than the bodies of people who die with their blood still in them.

At six in the morning, two pots on the fire, my mom was in the kitchen where she would be all day long making lard.

"Before washing, go start the willow smoke under the sausages", she said, and I read the accusation in her voice, her shame that I was already 14 and I constantly refused to do chores, favoring my reading. The revolution and its broadcast on television were, for my mom, the worst things to happen that year. Not that she didn't welcome the change, she did, but all that TV broadcasting made it difficult for her to ask for our help in the kitchen.

Traditional fruitcakes had to be made that December 23rd, other cakes and biscuits, too, and everything had to be done before the sun went down. Next day, on Christmas Eve, people would flock to our door and kids would sing carols and she would serve everyone fruitcake and cookies and home made biscuits. The kids would get tea and the adults red wine. And the wine was another problem. My dad had no time to take care of it so I had to go down to the basement and fill 10 or so bottles of wine from the huge 50 liter glass vat. In that vat the grape juice turned into wine in late autumn, and I put the wine-filled bottles in the pantry ready to be emptied by the thirsty carol singers.

Kids in the morning, youngsters in the evening and adults at night. I rushed outside into the cold, holding a newspaper and matchsticks for lighting the fire, under the sausages, then covering it with sawdust, wondering if carol singers would come.

I usually sang carols with my sister at Auntie Anişoara and Uncle Lulu's house, but not that year, I understood it wasn't allowed. Their house was across the street from the Town Hall, the place where Avrig's own Revolution continued, with Mr. Tatu as leader, and my father starting to make himself useful with his radio on which he spoke with the military operators in Sibiu.

As the willow smoke engulfed the meats, I returned to the kitchen only to discover my father packing a sandwich for work and my mom weighting flour. The kitchen scale was set to 3 kilograms and I knew that she was preparing to make the fruitcakes.

"Lucky you, Dad!" I said and he replied:

"Some day this'll be you!", and he smiled. He was lucky indeed. Although I didn't know why, the whole situation was funny for my mom too. She smiled while pointing to a bag full of nuts.

"I need them before noon". It was decided. No arguments, and as I saw my father leaving for the Town Hall, in his navy blue raincoat, one size bigger than mine, which I got the same time as his, I fixed my breakfast from last night's leftovers, sat at the table and started to devour it, mouth open, making noises to piss my mom off - my revenge for the bag of nuts.

After breakfast I had to wash the dishes my father and I had used. I needed the sink for the nuts. In the Romania of 1989 nuts for traditional fruitcakes didn't come from supermarkets in sealed plastic bags, but straight from the trees. We had a nut tree at the end of the garden.

"This tree grows tall and it makes a shade. I shall put it here", my grandfather had said, "to let our neighbors enjoy its nuts too", and he planted it so we could get only a quarter of all the nuts it produced, while the two neighboring gardens would get the rest of them. They were good nuts, bigger than the Kiku's, a neighbouring family.

The nuts rolled into the sink and I turned on the hot water tap. The gas boiler came to life and I could feel the water getting hotter and hotter. Then, I turned the boiler's dial to the hottest setting and with a wooden spoon I started to mix the nuts. Steam and their characteristic perfume spread throughout the house. I waited and after several minutes when they were well soaked I turned off the water.

My mom handed me an empty plastic bucket which I filled with the nuts. Soaked in hot water they would be easier to crack and clean. This was not an easy job and I wanted to do whatever I could to lessen my pain.

To crack nuts, people from the "civilized world" would use a nutcracker. I knew that there were nutcrackers in the world. I had once seen a ballet by Tchaikovsky with that name. But I had no idea what a nutcracker looked like. Nobody in my town did. All my friends cracked their nuts for their fruitcakes the same way I did: With a hammer and anvil.

So I had to set up my work space, and I took a small anvil that we always used from the kitchen and a common midsized hammer upstairs together with an old tablecloth. Since the dining table was still in my room, I wanted to work there and watch the Revolution while cracking the nuts.

First I woke up my sister and asked her to go downstairs to have her breakfast. During holidays we almost never had breakfast together but my mom did not care. We did have to eat lunch and supper together. Our parents always had breakfast without us, at 6 am, one hour before we would wake up. Their jobs started at 7 am so they had to wake up early every day. With Felicia gone, I turned on the TV and it was like the TV hadn't been turned off at all. It was like watching a rented videotape from the position you left it the previous night.

The same people were still there on the same screen, more tired than when they first entered the studio, but still the same. It was like they were afraid that they would lose their share of the new power if they left. Still, seeing them was comforting. It meant that Ceaușescu wasn't back and we were still fighting him. It also meant that the Arab terrorists trained by Ceaușescu weren't as powerful as everyone had feared. That morning I thought that despite seeing that the shooting was still going on we were about to win our freedom at last.

Did German kids crack nuts for their fruitcakes? I doubted it. I once saw in a German magazine a picture with fruitcakes that looked so much like ours, and I imagined how delicious they were and how easy to get from the stores. Instead, I had to work for mine, and I wasn't so happy about that.

I took a blanket and spread it on the dining table. On it I put the old table cloth and while sitting down I placed the anvil in front of me. The blanket was to protect the dining table but also to deaden the sound. If I wanted to watch TV the nut cracking had to be as quiet as possible.

Bang, bang. The hammer would hit the nut first lightly and then decisively. Bang, bang. Minding not to hit my fingers, bang, bang. I would continue until a pile of cracked nuts had accumulated and then stop and take the nuts out of their shells.

My sister came in and began to help me which I was grateful for. I got on with smashing and cracking the nuts while she took on the job of cleaning the nuts from the smashed shells. We were such a good team.

It was then that we heard that the Otopeni airport had been attacked by terrorists and the brave soldiers defending the building were fighting back. And we cheered. Me, especially, I was so proud of our great Army. So proud.

Proud also were the soldiers who opened fire on the three trucks and the civilian bus that came to attack them.

They were proud but they weren't free. They were nothing like private Radutoiu. Back in 1944 he was as young as they were when, as a private, he was parachuted into the war near Odessa, on the Eastern Front where Romanians and Germans were fighting a lost battle against the Soviet Red Army. When he left the plane he had two items with him: an assault rifle and a Bible. Before reaching the ground he had already dropped his rifle. "Why?" was my question when he told me that story the very first time. "Because written in my Bible was THOU SHALT NOT KILL. It was my choice," he said, and he didn't realize it but he was giving me the same definition of freedom that that French guy called Sartre coined after WWII was over. Private Radutoiu started to walk home, a small village in Oltenia, the very moment his feet touched the ground. And turning his back on the war he choose to be free.

"What happened next, did you make it home?" I asked.

"Yes, of course. God was with me. The next day I ran into some Russians. There I was, Bible in hand, looking for plants or fruits I could eat when I saw, not more than 50m away in a ravine, a tank. A T34. Waiting. They saw me, too, because the tank started to turn slowly in my direction. Boom, boom, boom. They were firing a heavy machine gun, but I'm not sure they really wanted to hit me because I wasn't hit. So I started to run, and ran under a tree. See, there were almost no trees in Odessa, except the huge one I was running towards, and the Russians behind me were boom, boom, boom. I prayed to God and got behind the tree and the tree was shaking. Boom, boom, boom. And I heard the tank moving, getting closer but I stayed there and didn't move. And the tank got so close I could hear them laughing and then it stopped and someone shouted something at me so I came out from behind the tree. Bible in hand. And we looked at each other. They were no younger nor older than I. Just like me, but dressed different. And then the tank started to move, turning away and I was left alone. I guessed that it was a good idea I dropped my rifle", he smiled, visibly satisfied with that outcome.

"So, how did you get across all that land to Oltenia?" I asked him again, expecting more miracles, but he caught me by surprise when he said:

"On my horse!"

"Your horse? You had no horse, you jumped from a plane, Bible and assault rifle only, no horse", I said in disbelief.

"Yes, I had my Bible. And I was getting close to the Dniester river. It's a huge river, you know. And there were other soldiers too. Maybe running home, like me, or retreating to other positions. I didn't ask. They didn't tell. But there was also a Wehrmacht officer. He was riding a superb horse, but he couldn't cross the river on it. So he set the horse free and jumped in the river and swam for half an hour to reach the other side. I was watching. And he got there and called the horse, but the horse didn't move. That was the moment I knew that horse was mine. God Himself was giving me a horse, and I called it as we called our horses back home, and the horse came. And I got on it and jumped in the river, and in less than 10 minutes we were already on the other side".

"And the Wehrmacht officer?" I asked eagerly.

"He came to me and said that that horse was his, but I answered in German 'You're wrong, Herr Officer. Your horse is on the other side of the river. This is my horse. If you want it we can swim back and you can bring it over'. He had a pistol, like all Wehrmacht officers, but I wasn't afraid. I was holding my dry Bible in my hand, and the officer saw it and smiled and asked me to take care of that horse...even now, after more than 50 years I pray for him and thank God he abandoned that beautiful horse...How proud I entered my village riding it" he said finishing his story.

As I told you before, the killers at the Otopeni Airport were proud too. And the truth is they stayed proud until they went outside to kill what was left of their 'attackers'. "Take no prisoners", was the order, and they were about to execute it when they saw that something was wrong. Terribly wrong. So they dropped the order and took prisoners. The terrorists were just a bunch of butchered kids, and they started to yell at and accuse them:

"You are terrorists, you came here to kill us", they yelled and they even hit them in the face with their AKM's, and blood was spilled inside the airport building, but the 'terrorists' were afraid. They looked at them with abject terror in their young eyes, so the brave Romanian soldiers who decimated half of them minutes before were not so proud anymore. Why did they shoot their guns? Nobody directly threatened their lives. Of course the orders were clear. The orders came from the top and they were classified. Three trucks full of terrorists dressed like army recruits were about to come and try to kill them. Nobody was to be taken alive but these were no terrorists. They were real recruits, they knew that but they were still angry. They had killed innocent people, so they continued to yell at them.

Guns were cocked, adrenaline was flowing in their veins and still floating inside their heads was the doubt: what if that fucker Ceauşescu trained kids as terrorists, what if these were, as the intelligence they had gotten indicated, real terrorists bent on taking revenge? So they stopped them from helping the wounded and it was then that Private Buta died like a pig. Some of those that had survived despite being critically wounded were lucky that a taxi driver drove by, stopped and took them to the hospital, away from the killers inside the airport, away from the dying Private Buta.

That taxi driver definitely had good karma. Snipers saw him picking up the bodies but they let him pick them up and drive away. He wasn't aware of it, but someone at the top in the Ministry of Defense had decided some wounded soldiers, possibly dead soldiers, paraded in a taxi through the crowds and then in hospitals would show that terrorists existed and that the new power was fighting them off. So he drove away, speaking to the wounded soldiers like the father he was. But I didn't know all that, and was still thinking about those German fruitcakes that I had only seen in photos. I was grateful for the job done by the Airport defenders.

Now I know, that was how I was supposed to feel. That was how the new leadership had planned it, it was just like General Militaru had imagined it. So I looked at Iliescu and Roman with adulation, and I loved them and prayed for them and wished them all the strength and good luck they needed in their fight against Ceauşescu.

How was I supposed to know that my prayers were already answered? How was I supposed to know Ceauşescu had been captured one day before when his capturers played with us and were pretending, on national television, that they were still hunting him down? How was I supposed to know there were no terrorists fighting for Ceauşescu but only brave soldiers fighting against invisible terrorists? And killing youngsters dressed in our country's wet uniforms?

In Sibiu the Securitate troops locked their guns in the basement the moment the Revolution started while the army attacked their building and completely destroyed it. Nobody shot at the army in Sibiu but the army shot at everyone. Anyone moving at night was a suspect, old foes were targeted..."Shoot at will", was the order and they all wanted to be brave. All the soldiers had brave hearts and wanted to kill their invisible enemy. The army captain that fired a rocket propelled grenade from inside a toilet was an idiot, of course, he got badly injured, but a hero, no more, no less. He rose in the ranks after the Revolution ended and, having been injured "in action", got financial benefits too.

Bang, bang.

I was still cracking the nuts and my sister was still helping me when at the airport the brave hearts, the cold-blooded killers who would also claim to be heroes, finally understood what had happened. They could see themselves being punished and tried to cover up their attack, so they made the survivors collect the bodies. But they were too late and the bodies were rigid. Frozen in the exact position they had fallen when the bullets sprayed through their bodies. They were unceremoniously piled on a truck. Small pieces were picked up too. And nobody really understood why, but the truck that took them to the city morgue got back too quickly.

The soldiers driving the truck were ordered to get rid of the "evidence" and when they said they did, their superiors were satisfied. General Militaru was satisfied, so they could take a rest and drink the brandy they had smuggled into their unit a few days earlier. But the truth is that they had failed. All the 48 bodies, Private Buta included, were supposed to disappear but they didn't have the guts to do it, so they abandoned the bodies, a grotesque pile, on a forklift inside the Cargo Terminal of the same Otopeni Airport. The workers arriving at work in the terminal on the morning of 25th of December, a Monday, discovered the frozen and inanimate pile and people were talking about terrorists. Nobody told them, "We did it!" or "We are sorry!"

Why would they? It was like a nightmare, and sooner or later nightmares are forgotten. No one had a Bible in their hands. Romania was secular. They didn't fight to get rid of Ceauşescu so they could read the Bible. Rather to drink Coca-Cola...

It was still morning when, thanks to my sister, I finished with the nuts. So I took them downstairs and grated them so that my mom could mix them with sugar, lemon juice and cocoa powder. Felicia was following with the hammer, the small anvil and the tablecloth.

The lard looked good in those huge pots. At 6 in the morning there were only white pieces of fat in them, but now those pieces of fat were fried pork rinds.

"Hey, those look good!" I said and planned to have some with sliced onions and white bread for lunch. So my mom gave me a look that said despite the Revolution happening outside our gates, we still had to fast, but I no longer cared. Like my father and sister's, my diet had changed since the pig's funeral feast. I took one rind, dipped it in salt, and slid it into my mouth.

Heavenly. Mom was consumed with her pots so she saw nothing.

To tell you the truth, the lard was a tough business. First of all, the quantities were huge. Secondly, you had to take care not to over fry it. From the beginning my mom had put water in the pots and she had to make sure some water always remained in the pots until the end. Otherwise the taste would be ruined. My dad used to say, and he was right, that overheated pig fat turned toxic, so we had to take care, which we did. My mom always carefully watched the lard until the end. When it was done, after turning off the fire, she fished out the pork rinds and put them in a traditional pot made of ceramic so it would look good when the rinds would be brought from the pantry for breakfast or dinner.

The phone rung once. My mom picked it up and turned white. She sat down and went "uh, uh" for about 10 minutes, then said, "Take care" and hung up.

On the other end of the line was Auntie Anişoara. Moments before revolutionaries at the Town Hall, as drunk as the day before, stormed their house looking for my father. It turned out that my father was doing what he always did, taking his break in his sister's house. Why? Because he always got real hot coffee there - in those days the nearby coffee shop only served substitutes - and because he could use a clean toilet. He was, at 39 years old, still Auntie Anişoara's little brother.

But the revolutionaries didn't know my father's habits and they assumed he was trying to contact terrorists over the phone and give them information about how many people were defending the Town Hall, in order to get everyone killed.

It was all paranoia, the same paranoia that gripped the minds of the defenders of the Otopeni Airport, but nobody was able to reason. My auntie said that my dad was lucky. He was caught sipping coffee while cheering about the news on the success of those defending Otopeni. And the revolutionaries got happy, too, and they were invited to sit down and have some coffee, which they did. They were served cakes and finally they left with my father as their friend and not as their enemy to do revolutionary things that my auntie did not understand inside the Town Hall.

My mom was quite upset.

It was Uncle Ion's fault, once again, and she had seen it coming since she heard about the Velvet Revolution in Czechoslovakia. Now that her worst fears had turned into an ugly reality, she felt desperate.

Uncle Ion was my father's older brother. My grandfather wanted him to become a priest. We were Greek orthodox so our priests marry, and, in a time when almost all Romanians were farmers and had no other wishes than continuing farming, my grandfather paid huge amounts of money to give Uncle Ion an education. The best education available. Violin lessons included, Uncle Ion went to high school in Sibiu when WWII started, but when it ended, with communists taking over the country, the king going into exile and priests being hunted down and imprisoned, my grandfather's dream was shattered.

But with his background as a half farmer the communists took Uncle Ion and made him an army officer and in a few years he was in the Secret Police, the infamous Securitate, working in intelligence, defending his country. Or so was the story. Did he do bad things in Fagaras where he was based? I don't know. He never told his family what he was doing and nobody asked questions, in return. And with that status quo we had lived many years.

But now that the regime change was upon us and the Securitate was blamed for everything that had gone wrong in Romania in the past 40 and something years, people remembered. People remembered who the Securitate officers were, who their kin were, and my mom hated being related to Uncle Ion. She didn't like them, Uncle Ion and Aunt Dorina. Unlike Uncle Lulu who visited us every second day, we used to see Uncle Ion only twice a year. He lived in a flat in Sibiu, 20 km from our house, and came to visit only for the pig.

Until my grandfather's death we used to keep three pigs. One for us, one for Uncle Ion and one that my grandfather would share with Uncle Lulu.

"Mommy, when you're old we'll raise you a pig every year", Aunt Dorina said to my grandmother every time they met. "We'll visit you and bring you sweets", she used to go on, but it never happened. My grandmother was already old when Aunt Dorina was promising sweets, more than 70, and she had diabetes. They hardly ever came and when they did they were always empty handed. And, after 1987 when Uncle Ion had that stroke that left him half paralyzed, they stopped coming at all. In 1989 when my grandfather died, only my cousin, Ioan, their only spoiled child, came to the funeral service. Aunt Dorina refused to let her husband know of his father's death. She didn't want to "shock him". And she didn't shock him with the news of my grandmother's death either, in 1994, nor with the news of my father's death, a year later in 1995.

Although half paralyzed, Uncle Ion wasn't stupid, so he figured out that his closest kin had died but they told him first stories of hospitals and disease and only later when they couldn't lie anymore, the truth. But it was always too late. For him and for us. It was said that all Securitate big shots "had strokes" when they retired. They knew too much. This was only the second positive thing about Uncle Ion I could think of. The first is when I was a first grader in Elementary school and got hepatitis, he came to my mom and gave her one liter of olive oil. That was the first and the last time before 1989 we saw olive oil. He asked my mom to cook with it for me because, sick as I was, my liver would accept it better than the lard we used to eat. One liter of olive oil... The good in him loved his little brother, and in return my father worshiped him too. He would visit his brother every time he was in Sibiu and he would tell me that he grew up on Uncle Ion's shoulders. So many forests my Uncle had crossed with his little brother around his neck in the early 50's that my father learned those forests well before he learned his way to school.

I remember Uncle Ion as an overweight officer, with black sunglasses, carrying a hunting gun every time he stopped to visit.

"Can you shoot our dog? It's too noisy", our neighbors once asked him, and I now suspect they were insane, and he did. He called to the white dog to come and sit. "Roll over", he said, and the dog was playful and rolled over. So he put the rifle's nuzzle into the dog's ear and before I could close my eyes I heard a bang, and the dog's ear filled up with blood. My neighbor said, "Thank you!" and served us drinks. Then he took his dead dog and dumped it on the river bank to rot.

One liter of olive oil… I remember it came in a moss green can, and my mom used it as if it were something sacred and she cooked separate food for me and I got well.

But one liter of olive oil could not pay for all the shit my mom had to take from her brother-in-law's wife. After her marriage with my father, unapproved by Uncle Ion, Aunt Dorina had the crazy idea that, since my dad would inherit the house he shared with my grandparents, the young couple should pay compensation to Uncle Ion and Aunt Anişoara. And at a time when combined my dad and my mom made just 2000 lei, they had to pay 10,000 lei to each of his siblings. Maybe she hated my mom because she broke her leg during their wedding party, stepping on some cherries that someone had dropped on the floor. Who knows?

And then there were the pigs my parents were slaving over- always given as presents. And the wine, and the homemade brandy, and the cereals too. I wonder now how my mom didn't go crazy when my dad always accepted whatever his father, brother or sister said? Was it that she loved him so much or was it that she understood that my father was 20 years younger than his siblings, always a child in their eyes?

I do not know for sure, but I know and I knew back then in 1989 that a relative in the Securitate, even a retired one with a poison pill in his mouth, was bad karma for us. Worse, we may suffer, despite the fact that we didn't get along very well.

It turned that Aunt Dorina was scared by the terrorists too. And the people in their building, many of them linked with the army or with the Securitate, barricaded the entrance of their building and discussed what to do if terrorists came and attacked them. So they decided to get those with hunting rifles on the roof as guards. My cousin Ioan was one of them, and he stood on that roof, rifle in hand, until my uncle heard where his spoiled son was, and in broken words – he had a speech impediment after he was paralyzed – he ordered him to come down before being spotted by the real terrorists or the Army hunting for terrorists.

I was bringing the pots with the fried ribs and my mom was filling them up with hot lard, when the phone rung again. I picked up and it was that drunk voice I was expecting the most: our family's godson.

"Open the gate, if you have it closed, I'm coming with the tree", he said and I was already running. Finul (godson in Romanian) Moisică presented us, every year, with a Christmas tree. He had access to the forest where he did jobs for the forestry department using his own horse and cart. Our friends, who got their trees in the market, always envied us for the beauty of ours. But with the Revolution, I was fearing we would have to give up on having a beautiful tree that year and go buy an ugly one, the kind that Ceaușescu could not export to other countries, or worse, not have a Christmas tree at all.

I opened the gate and went back to the kitchen where my mom asked me to fetch some brandy. Finul Moisică was a heavy drinker. With the brandy on the table we kept bringing pots with ribs or just empty pots until the lard was all in the pantry, waiting to save the day, during the following year. Finul Moisică didn't come until my mom finished washing the pots. I was moving the second one back into the basement and thinking I would check the willow smoke under the sausages, when he entered our front yard carrying a silver Christmas tree.

"Thank you, thank you", I ran out to greet him and he proudly put the tree in the snow, before he entered the house where he had all the brandy in the bottle.

"I must go now, my horses are getting cold", he said, and took his handmade whip that I so much admired and went out onto the street where the two horses waited impatiently. He climbed into the cart and showed them the whip but he didn't have to use it, he never did, they were already galloping homeward. "It doesn't matter how drunk I get, once in my carriage my horses take me home" he once said, and that must have been the truth because from where I was standing before closing the gate, he didn't look like he was steering them.

Before going back to the kitchen where my mom was about to ask for help with the fruitcakes, I climbed under the roof to find the Christmas Tree stand. Unused all year, sometimes it got rusty. But I was lucky that year. I found it dirty but otherwise in good shape.

I took it downstairs, washed it and poured boiling water on it. It was my mother's idea of cleanliness and since we took our shoes off before entering the house – the kitchen an exception – I guess that the boiling water was another Japanese thing that she loved without being herself Japanese.

In the kitchen mom was dissolving beer yeast in lukewarm milk. In Romania yeast came in 500 gram packs which resembled over-sized pieces of butter, not in powder form as it usually comes in the rest of the world. When buying such a yeast pack we would cut it in 20 pieces, 25 grams per piece, and freeze them until they were needed. On the table I could count 3 pieces of white paper, one piece for each kilo of flour that we had weighed before. Twenty years after the Revolution yeast, usually imported, is sold dry in small plastic packages. Only when she's lucky can my mom get her favorite real yeast. And then her fruitcakes grow as they used to when Ceauşescu was still alive and we just small children that knew no other sweets other than those we helped my mother make.

The milk was brought out, put in a pot which my mom put close to the stove. A bottle with sunflower oil with which we would rub our hands was brought out too. The oil rubbing was to prevent the dough from sticking to our fingers.

The flour was in a very large bowl so, after washing my hands carefully in hot water, I made a hole in the middle of it in which my mom started to break eggs. On the eggs went some sugar, a big spoon of salt, lemon peel and the yeast smelling lukewarm milk. First with big folding movements then, as the flour started to stick to my fingers, with shorter but taster strokes, I kneaded the dough. Three kilograms of flour is a lot to knead and for that reason it wasn't the job of a single person. The kneading would have to last for more than an hour, so it was an impossible task for just one of us to do alone.

I started as usual and continued until I couldn't anymore and handed it over.

When mom was younger and I was yet unable help her, she would have finished kneading in half an hour or so, but then our fruitcake wasn't as good as Aunt Anişoara's was. That was until they told us their secret which was that they took turns kneading, for an hour or so.

It was getting painful. Eventually I couldn't move my hands without moving the whole kneading bowl so I asked for help.

"I'm sorry about this year's oranges", my mom said without looking at me.

"With all this fighting going on I'm afraid we won't be able to get oranges at all", and I was right, she was sour, and sad.

We worshipped oranges. Bananas too.

In 1989 we had food coupons, something that people in the Western World probably had during WWII, but those coupons were just for bread, sugar and oil. Not for oranges, not for bananas or anything else.

Usually just before Christmas, all orange worshippers gathered in front of the one and only food store in that town – and I cannot call that Alimentara a supermarket, nor I can call it a grocery store, it mostly sold alcohol and sardines in oil – and waited. For hours or for days. When they were tired and wanted to sleep they would leave their bags on the pavement to wait for them. And then, the next day at 5 in the morning, or even earlier, they would go and stand in that line again, and they would continue to do that ritual until the divine oranges would show their orange light in that dark store.

Now I can close my eyes and see that Alimentara and the people waiting outside and it's not just an impression, but the real thing, the real gray thing, and all I can think is that our life in communism was colorless. We had no colors during winter, the snow was white only for a couple of days, but we had gray, lots of gray and mud, and when we were lucky the mud was frozen and it was so cold that we were spared the smell of the other orange worshippers that gathered for days just to be able to touch the color of countries with no lines for food and no secret police.

My father was usually the one who fought the cold and the body odors to get us oranges.

"Only five each! Only five each!", was the yell that replaced the nonexistent "Welcome!". And if you could picture the dirty and arrogant shopkeepers and the hungry and desperate crowd that waited outside for a couple of days or more you can only agree with the revulsion of Ceaușescu's wife, Elena. When she saw a similar line for food, she said to our Great Nation's leader "Look at those worms! They're like worms on carrion!". She was partly right. When the state didn't provide hot water in winter people smelled like worms on a corpse.

"Only five each!" and my father would bring home just five oranges and five bananas. And we would keep them in our room, the kids room, and life became so much brighter.

The bananas would change color from that green that only bananas have to a bright yellow, and we would eat them over the next ten days. One day a banana, one day an orange, until we had no more and life was gray again as it usually was from the 5th of January, the last day of our winter celebrations, John the Baptist's day, to the Ignat's Day, pig slaughtering day, on December 20th.

"Christmas without the smell of oranges is not the Christmas I was looking for", I said in a fake happy voice not wanting to make mom suffer more than she already was, but I got no reply. I guess I shouldn't have said that. That year we could not do our orange worshipping ritual of cutting the oranges and eating them while beautifully preserving their skins.

Maybe you've seen it, maybe not, maybe you've done it, maybe not, but to peel an orange and leave behind a beautiful flower you just need a sharp knife and some patience. First, with a single cut you open the orange across the bottom. Then cut the skin with vertical strokes from that open bottom to 3cm from the top. You can go on 6 to 8 times, depending on how big the orange is, and then start to peel while keeping the skin in one piece. The final result is an empty orange which we used to display in an empty glass, and day by day we would watch its color with hope, without knowing that 15 years later in Romania another "revolution" would take place, the Orange Revolution. The people voted massively against the former communists who were not expelled from power in the bloody events of 1989, but rather reconfirmed in it.

We displayed those orange skins every year, until they turned into flowers, and threw them out only in early summer, when their orange color would have turned dark and not be a pleasant sight anymore.

I was still thinking about oranges and bananas when my mom changed places with me and furiously continued to knead the dough. She was so much more experienced and it seemed fun and easy. I was sure it was not. I needed all my strength to keep the kneading bowl in place, while my mother's hands performed like an industrial dough kneading machine we used to see on the news, almost every day.

What a country of masochists Romania was... The sadistic TV crews always showed collective farms producing even more food and Romania ranked number five in wheat exports in the world, but we had to buy bread with coupons!

My dad stood in line once a year for our oranges and bananas, but I stood in line almost every day for bread. For one hour, for two hours, three, for as long as it took.

The bread shop was run by Mrs Presecan, a soft looking, stocky lady in her 40's. She would wait from morning to early afternoon in her empty store where she had nothing to sell, while people started to gather outside. It was always better to get there early, but with school, lunch, chores and friends wanting to play, it was impossible most of the time, so I usually ended up around halfway down from the top of the line. And while there, shorter than the adults around me, I used to listen to their talk, usually local gossip, sometimes political jokes, sometimes food recipes, and constantly move my weight from one foot to the other, watching the ground for familiar looking stones, following with my eyes ants that had already got food for their homes...

"Half of their lives people just wait", comforted my father when I used to complain, and I guess he was right. I was always waiting for something. Thinking about countries that I had visited in the books I had read, or in my dreams after listening to people talking about them.

And then the bread truck would show up, and people would push towards the shop doors, pushing and kicking their way, not thinking about the kids standing in line. Sometimes without once touching the ground with my feet I was carried in and out, but that was life and I had to buy bread, my family trusted me to do it. I had no other choice.

The truck always came down the road and then turned around in the middle of the street, hitting the breaks when its rear was parallel with the bread shop door.

And the driver and the other deliveryman would get out and the people push with even more impatience. But they would first smoke their stinky cigarettes, and then, just before the crowd was going to literally go crazy they would open the back doors. Round bread would shine from inside the truck and no matter how powerful the sunshine was, to us the bread shined even stronger.

Its perfume however was more hypnotic than its shining and suffocating inside that pack of hungry adults I could hear stomachs protesting and, as the two deliverymen started to unload the truck all conversations ceased, fists clenched exact change, hands got the bread coupons ready for stamping.

If you think that unloading a truck full of bread takes time, you're wrong! It doesn't. Or at least it didn't back in 1989 when the deliverymen would take the boxes full of bread and empty them on the floor, creating a pile of bread that almost filled up the small bread shop.

Mrs Presecan stood behind the counter, knife ready.

When I first visited Germany and France I saw that only some bakers had knives on the counters and only in very expensive bakeries where customers would choose to buy a cut of bread instead of the whole thing. But Mrs Presecan's shop wasn't a posh German bakery and we didn't buy part loaves because it was our choice.

On our monthly bread coupon was written the amount we would get. We didn't want to buy less, and we couldn't buy more, so Mrs Presecan's knife had to slice bread in quarters or thirds every time she couldn't sell full loaves.

Often the bread picked up from the floor was dirty, but when you get a dirty loaf you can always dust it as you do a dirty cloth.

"Three and a quarter loaves, please", I used to say and hand over my coupon to be stamped and the right change, never bills. Before my grandfather died in 1987 I used to say "Three and a half loaves, please", and it was like my grandfather was supposed to eat only a quarter of a loaf, nothing more, nothing less.

Three and a quarter loaves was the amount that a family of two adults, two kids and a grandmother was entitled to buy in communist Romania. I am glad I didn't think so much about it at the time. I could have easily gone crazy, as other people did, and do or say things that may have gotten us imprisoned or even killed.

"Can I have one more today?" I was speaking at once with shame and fear. "We have guests today". I was ashamed. The people around me would think that if Mrs Presecan granted my request, people at the end of the line would go to their kids empty handed. The fear was because I always knew there was the possibility that I wouldn't get the desired bread and we wouldn't be able to feed our guests as we were supposed to.

Suddenly my mom straightened her back. The dough was ready. It looked and smelled good. She covered it with a white piece of cloth and then asked me to wash my hands.

The bowl with the dough was covered sitting on a chair, right in the middle of the kitchen. That image was so familiar to me and always so new. Before my grandfather's death, my granny used to bake bread twice a week. Her bread was much tastier than what we had to eat that Christmas. But 1986 was the last year we got our share of wheat from the CAP, the Romanian version of the Soviet kolkhoz, and in early 1987 the mill stopped milling wheat. It didn't close. That mill had a line for corn, too, but why would I care about that?

No wheat to mill no flour to buy, no bread to bake. It was a few months before my grandfather died that my parents decided to rebuild that section of our house which housed the kitchen and in the process we demolished our oven and with it a huge part of our lifestyle.

It didn't seem important to me at the time to rebuild a traditional wood burning oven, but afterwards, when we couldn't eat oven-dried prunes or oven-dried pears, or have fruitcakes baked in that oven, life became duller than before.

"If you rebuild the house, I will surely die", said my grandfather to my dad, and we all looked at him in sympathy. Despite not showing much of the 82 years he had lived before 1986, his age was catching up with him and he was, as always, right. He died in 1987 of pulmonary cancer. The doctors tried to cure an ulcer he had on his ear with radiation, and they exposed him to too much. He died coughing up his lungs, but his ear was just fine. A huge victory for the doctor that cured him.

It was late afternoon and he was lying in his bed, the whole family around him, to be with him, to hear his stories. Simion Grancea had only 8 years of formal schooling. But his father was a sergeant in the Austro-Hungarian Imperial Army and he wanted to pass away with dignity.

"I guess that I'd be an old fool to say au revoir", he said in a low voice and everybody understood at once what was about to happen. "Can I have a last moment to myself?" he asked again and without waiting for a response he turned away from us and we distinctly heard his last breath.

Two days later, when his body was laid in the coffin in our front room and I got a few moments alone with him I touched his cold hand that used to take me so many times to see the trains. I promised I would leave Avrig and go further than anyone in our family ever had, so the people of the world, the free world, would hear my name, his name and see how noble his kin was, is. Our nickname was "The Sergeants" and we were proud...

But then, how could we possibly have known that rebuilding that part of the house would kill my grandfather? He had said the same when he planted that walnut tree at the end of the garden: "When this tree is as wide as my chest I will die", and that tree was as wide as his chest for as long as I can remember...

Who could have known?

The third day after he died I got a day off school. I was at Mrs Presecan's bread shop in the morning, waiting for the bread truck. I was there with Uncle Lulu and his car, a forest green Dacia 1300 with a French engine. Uncle Lulu was an accountant at the Glass Factory and had some leverage everywhere so he placed a private order with the Bread Factory in Sibiu. We were there for 800 large butter rolls, 300g each, that we planned to give with handkerchief-wrapped candles to the mourners that would see Sergeant Simion off on his last journey.

And the truck came but there were no people to flock around and push to get into the small bread shop. Money changed hands and the truckers didn't throw the butter rolls on the floor but placed them carefully in Uncle Lulu's car.

Then out of nowhere Bogdan and Emil, my friends and classmates passed by and I rushed to them and gave them some butter rolls that they could eat with everybody else at school. Uncle Lulu scolded me. He feared we wouldn't have enough for all the mourners that would come. But my friends got the rolls and a few days later at school they were still talking about it like they were some kind of heroes. I felt that funerals definitely had some benefits, at least for those still living.

In the end, Uncle Lulu was almost right, but still, with fingers crossed, we had enough for everyone who came to pay their respects. "Odihneasca-se in pace" (Rest in peace), the people said, and those were exactly the same words that the bread deliverymen used as a goodbye.

The deliverymen moved on for they were late. That day everybody would wait an hour more in front of the bread shop, but not so impatient as usual. They would already have butter rolls at home thanks to their family members who had seen my grandfather off on his last journey.

Back upstairs Felicia was still watching the Revolution live on the blaring black and white TV. I was there only to steal a candy from the box with the Christmas tree ornaments. Those candies came wrapped in bright colored paper and their purpose was to hang in the Christmas tree. I remember that when I was little they used to be chocolate candies. Then, when I entered school in 1982 they turned in chocolate covered jelly, and then, after 86' they were just sugar candies. They could just as well use sugar candies, chocolate was too expensive for the people, Ceauşescu had thought one day...

But they were something I could play with. I had discovered that I could replace the candy inside the wrapper with a piece of paper, and the effect would be the same, so every now and then I was indulging myself in the sweets. Not as often as I wished. Those candies were supposed to last until the 5th of January, and dad would be concerned if he saw I was eating too much sugar.

It's strange that my mother agree with him. And even stranger was the fact that she was constantly making me sweets and buying acacia honey. Every day before going to bed, long after having brushed my teeth, she would give me a big spoon of honey, it was like a ritual, but a ritual that I so much enjoyed. And I was a healthy kid who had no cavities. They would come later, after leaving my house to go to high school in Sibiu where I switched from the healthy food I was used to, to the canteen and junk food that appeared on the market after the Revolution.

On the TV set the Revolutionaries were running the country. They were fighting from Studio 6 of the TV station and it appeared that the terrorists were trying to break in.

"The Russians just can't come", I said to my sister and started to remember the story that we were told so many times in school by our teacher. The story of how the Russians were camped in the Brukenthal palace in Avrig, and how over the winter they completely destroyed the place, burned down all the late 18th Century and early 19th Century antique furniture, how they stole everybody's long winter coats and watches.

"One day three soldiers went into that wine cellar and started to drink, and they got drunk and started to fire their guns and cracked a huge wine casket only to drown in it". That was the story. The true one. But the Russian commander said that his men had been intentionally drowned and the cellar's owner was shot and buried like a common thief while those three drunks were put in the same cemetery as war heroes.

Those were tough times and I really hoped we wouldn't have to live through such times.

But hard times were to come. We didn't know it yet, the people on the TV screen were only impostors. Starting with Iliescu, the apparatchik that wanted to be our Gorbachev, with Petre Roman, the son of Walter Roman, the very Jew that came from Moscow in a Soviet tank to install the communist regime in Bucharest, along with his friend and Jew, Ana Pauker, with General Stănculescu, house man of the Ceaușescus.

They were there to stop us from living our democratic dreams, to stop us from reforming the country. When the Czechs sold their Skoda enterprises to Volkswagen in Germany for 1 Deutchemark, Romanians were fooled by Iliescu and Roman into shouting "We don't sell our country". And we didn't. We gave it for free to the people on that TV screen and their families and friends. And they did with what they got the only thing they could have done. Destroyed everything and started a sale.

Maybe worse than the Russians, the deep economic crisis that followed in the early 90's, with sky rocketing inflation, brought us stress and despair. But I didn't know that those things would come. Neither did the soldiers defending the TV station from the invisible terrorists. With one exception they all looked like kids and most of them were malnourished after so many months in our glorious shovel and plough wielding Army.

That one exception was a big, well-fed soldier, defending the TV tower with only a small handgun. "You're so fucking big, why don't you have a bigger gun?" a captain asked him. "Give him a machine gun!" the captain barked the order to his unit leader, and he got the biggest machine gun on that barricade. He felt so proud carrying it and shooting it in the night towards the invisible terrorists. How was he supposed to know that twenty years later he would be the biggest Romanian ever? Weighting almost 400 kilos, with a waist line of more than 2 meters, shitting in a bucket because he couldn't fit into the bathroom? When he was shooting the machine-gun he was under the illusion he was getting the terrorists. But the real terrorists were the people he was defending, and his biggest foe was capitalism. Its junk food, its Coca-Cola and potato chips, the super-sized meals that he came to enjoy. His wife would cook every day as if it were Christmas day, forgetting the fasting and the simple way of life that they enjoyed before getting married, before Romanian communism met its end, before her husband started to grow bigger and bigger until he became trapped in their own living room.

Watching the Romanian Revolution live was exciting but we were getting tired. Many years later, I once rented the entire season 1 of "24", that blockbuster American drama, and watched it in 18 hours, and the feeling was exactly the same. It was exciting and interesting to watch but at the same time it was painful to continue watching it for so long.

That was why I left my sister with my grandmother to watch TV and went to the kitchen to see the fruitcake.

As I had been hoping the beer yeast had done its magic and now the kneading bowl looked like a balloon ready to burst. On the table the kneading board (a 1.5 meter wooden square) was already oiled. In all cook books I have read the same old advice of putting flour on the board when kneading and flattening dough. But this only increases the amount of flour in the dough, so we used oil instead.

Now it was time for some fun. Me and my mom took chunks of dough, flattened them on the board until less than 1cm thick and then covered them with ground nuts, cocoa powder and sugar, lemon peel in sugar, or, as a variation, raisins soaked in brandy with vanilla oil, or, yet another variation, diced Turkish jelly. Then we would roll the dough into a long cylinder shape and we would place it in a buttered rectangular cooking tin.

We had many cooking tins. We were always baking fruitcakes. Some of the fruitcakes went to another uncle of mine, my mom's half-brother, Vasile. He was an alcoholic who was always losing his job but who already had a family and three little girls. His wife was from Oltenia and they clearly were a good match. She never baked, so we felt that it was our duty to supply them with fruitcakes. We couldn't leave them have a Christmas table without Christmas cakes.

My mom phoned their neighbor and asked him to send her brother for the Christmas supplies later on that day. This was how things worked in Romania. Not many people had phones. The telephone company was completely analog and could not provide numbers for everyone.

When all the fruitcakes were in their tins I took the white tablecloth and covered them. Before we baked them they had to double in size. But I was patient. I knew I was close to eating some freshly made fruitcake. When I was younger, my mom never let me eat any before Christmas Eve, when she would cut two or three fruitcakes and get them ready for the carol singers. It was customary to serve them fruitcake, talk with them for a while and then give them money before they left, so everyone stopped fasting one day earlier than we were supposed to. But times had changed and I had stopped fasting on the day we slaughtered the pig. It was as if the pig came before Lord Jesus Christ as my angry grandmother had put it...Anyway, my mom always baked a smaller cake for me, along with a flat sweet cake that we would give to the young men from town late Christmas Eve, when they came to sing traditional Christmas carols.

Baking two fruitcakes at a time, my mom would be watching the oven late into the evening, so she was still doing it, and I was still eating my small fruitcake, from which I cut a slice for my sister, when my father came home.

He was happy to be with us again, in the kitchen, and he started to smoke one of his cigarettes and the smoke that I so much liked combined with the baking smells that were coming from the hot oven and that winter day of December 1989 looked so peaceful, so ordinary, such a precious Christmas moment.

We were almost free, my father told us, Ceauşescu was still on the run, he said, and of course he didn't know that he had already been a prisoner of Iliescu and his men for more than 24 hours.

That day someone had radioed from Sibiu that terrorists were about to attack Avrig, and the people in the city hall got anxious. My father was going for his coffee break at Auntie Anișoara's house, and they came after him believing that he was a traitor, but things settled down and Mr. Tatu called for calm. But then they had to send someone up the Church Tower to watch the road from Sibiu with a machine gun and the orders were to shoot at all suspicious looking cars.

The fact is that only two shots were fired that day but nobody was hit. The suspicious car was a car that somebody knew. And, as there were very few cars at the time, all of them were safe to drive without being shot at.

"What about other people just happening to pass by", I asked, and my father told me that if they flew the red, yellow and blue Romanian flag with the communist part cut out they would not be considered suspicious and be let through. And suddenly it occurred to me that either the revolutionaries were utterly stupid or the terrorists were. But again, I was quite young in 1989, and I didn't speak up so I wouldn't be considered naive.

My mother started to make cornulete. She would use lots of lard for those cookies. The dough would sit for one night in the cold pantry before being used and made into the most fabulous sweets in the world.

It's strange to think now of cornulete. The last time I had such treats was more than ten years before sitting down to write this book, but I cannot possibly think about that Revolution without my mouth watering at the thought of how good they were.

With nuts, with prune jam or with Turkish jelly, they were covered in powdered sugar so, when put in your mouth, they would stay hard for just a moment before melting into the most perfect sweet bite that one ever tasted. Their filling, the jam or the Turkish jelly would be the final reward, something that I always tried to keep in my mouth as long as possible before letting it go slowly down, a movement of the tongue and throat that had to be perfectly coordinated with the open mouth for the next cornulete. Strange as it is, I discovered recently, a long time after eating my mom's cornulete that the Chinese have a similar treat. It's a different shape and doesn't have the same filling as my mom put in hers, but no doubt about it, the same kind of dough. And I wasn't even as surprised as I was when I ordered a 55 proof Chinese brandy which came with a long name of 5 Chinese characters, only to discover it tasted like the one I used to make with my father from prunes kept in barrels in the sunshine until the fermentation processes made our courtyard smell of alcohol.

That evening I refused to eat supper with the rest of my family. I had had almost all the fruitcake that mom baked specially for me, and I was full. So, when my sister joined my grandmother and my parents in the kitchen for dinner, I stayed with the blaring TV. Of course the revolution was continuing, the shooting sound was still coming from the lone speaker that my Opera TV had, and the people on the screen looked sometimes brave, sometimes scared, sometimes tired. But all of them looked like they were fighting each other to be in the center of the screen, as close as possible to Ion Iliescu, our unelected new leader.

Later that day cousin Ioan would call us to tell us in a quite self-satisfied voice that he knew one of those people. It was the assassin-looking guy always standing beside Iliescu and his name was Dan Iosif. After the Revolution it was said that he was the one in the crowd who shouted "Down with Ceaușescu" and that he was among the first to enter the Central Committee building. People would go on to say that it was there he made his first million, looting Ceaușescu's foreign currency coffers.

It was dark outside and the lights were turned off. I was still alone in front of the TV, watching the Revolution with delight. School uniforms were to be abolished, they said. We could go to school in our own clothes! I was so happy.

One year on, I was a high school student in Sibiu and, being from a small town, I was the least well-dressed in my class. My parents had no money to buy me the fancy clothes my classmates were wearing and the girls never paid any attention to me. The other eight boys in my class didn't seem to be bothered about what I was wearing, until Bogdan, my best friend and half-Hungarian, now a trauma doctor, said "Stay away from Circo, he's always making fun of you", and he was right. Luckily, soon after Circo found the math and chemistry that we were doing too difficult for him, and moved to another class. At least, the small group of boys that remained, were all my friends, but the girls there never changed, always acting over precious, sadistic and cheap.

But again, on that 23rd of December 1989, the prospect of going to school without a uniform, for the first time in my life, was thrilling. My handmade Sunday clothes were both my mother's and my pride and joy. Everything she couldn't make we ordered at Mr. Bara's, Avrig's one and only tailor.

I was friend and classmate with his son, Ovidiu, a very good boy that used to beat me up every time he saw me in kindergarten, but who, only God knows why, turned into a compassionate and fight hating pupil.

When I think back to then, I think that I was quite fortunate to grow up near people like Mr. Bara. As a tailor he was one of only a handful of people in Avrig that were allowed by the communist state to have a private business. He worked at his home, 100 meters up the road from ours, and he would receive us, friends, neighbors and customers with candies and coffee. There, while waiting to be measured, or trying to see if pants would fit or asking him to make the ones that we were wearing a little bit longer, we could look at old German Nekerman magazines from which Mr. Bara used to get inspired when launching Avrig's latest exclusive fashion.

While he was tailoring pants and jackets and shirts and suits and dresses for wedding-goers, churchgoers and funeral-goers alike, my grandmother was tailoring leather to make sheepskin vests for the young men in our town.

Like Mr. Bara, my grandmother was a certified master craftsman.

In 1993 when she died she was working with her hand up in the air on an invisible vest and she knew she was dying and asked my mom, as she was suddenly aware of herself, to finish her work after she was gone.

Over the years she hopelessly and helplessly tried to get apprentices, but the girls that parents sent her always quit. They hated – because the communist government made them hate – anything traditional. They were peasant-born but somehow so similar in the way they thought to the girls in my posh high school. They all hated handmade things, they all wanted to dress like people in the West, like those that lived their lives from day one in democracies.

On that very evening my grandmother was eating downstairs with my sister, the grandchild that she loved more than her own sons. She liked my sister more than she liked me, that was a fact.

On the night I was born she came to Brukenthal palace, the same one devastated by Russian soldiers after WWII, and, because the rule was that nobody could enter the part of the Palace deliveries were carried out in, asked from the street: "What is it?"

"It's a boy", shouted my young and beautiful mom, from a high window, like those women with blue blood that delivered boys and girls there during the 19th Century, but my grandmother said "Not again!", in a very upset voice, and then she left, taking the handmade cake with her, not once looking back.

One year and a half my mom had to endure the chores and anger that grandmother prepared for her while she was walking away in the night from the Palace. I was her third grandson, born almost two decades after Uncle Ion gave her a grandson, Ioan and Auntie Anişoara, another one, Mihai. And she had waited all those years for a miracle, for a granddaughter and the granddaughter wouldn't come.

Her own daughter refused to become a traditional leather tailor, and that job was a job that only a woman could do. Another grandson was not what she had wanted, so when Felicia was born she fussed about her so much that I wasn't yet two when I attacked my sister's cradle with a stick and hit her face in an act of jealousy that now, as a parent myself, I can't imagine ever doing.

That December in 1989, my grandmother was so close to her dream coming true. She had taught my sister the fine art of needles and everything a young lady had to know, but Felicia was still a child. She was thin and didn't have the strength to work the needle on the sheep skin. Grandmother did everything by hand and had never heard of a leather tailor who had leather sewing machines. But my grandmother always thought in a couple of years Felicia would be strong enough.

She couldn't have known that the first lesson she gave my sister was also to be the last one. No leather, no sheep skins, no silk, no needles. The last leatherwork master in that area died at 90 years old a few years before and nobody wanted to take over his stinky, underpaid work. The industrial leather makers dyed the sheep skins while my grandmother wanted them white, or they did not use skins with wool, or they didn't bother to use sheep skin because shoes were made of pig's skin.

Afterwards, when she had gone senile, after being just sad, sometimes when I gave her lunch during the long summer holidays I had in high school, I thought of the senility not as a curse but a blessing. The young people of our town started to wear, even on Christmas, blue jeans jackets, instead of her traditional leather vests.

Yes, things changed rapidly after 1989. Borders opened and my father went to visit Turkey.

"When we got out of that bus we looked like a prune basket", he told me laughing bitterly at the fact that everybody in those days turned to jeans. How stupid I was to be happy to get rid of my school uniform when the entire country stupidly took on capitalism's Turkish counterfeit Levi's jeans.

The truth is that at that very moment I wasn't thinking about Levi's. Not even in my dreams did I see myself owning an original pair of jeans. I wasn't a doctor's son or an apparatchik's son. We were poor so we had to wear tailored clothes and there was no way around it.

However, the way they prepared the speech, with Iliescu in the middle, was obvious. They knew things that we didn't and they were about to tell us something any moment now.

"Something has happened! Dad, Felicia, mom, hurry up, something is going to be announced on the TV".

I was rushing back with my father, shoulder to shoulder, my sister trailing behind us, and we heard from the doorway "The dictator and his wife have been caught", and we shouted for joy. We were free.

"God help us, he won't reach a deal with the revolution", my father said, and as we listened the dictator was about to be put on trial for those thousands of people killed in Timişoara, for the crimes of communism and for keeping us in fear and hunger.

"Now, if only the Russians would stay out of it", he said and he nervously lit a cigarette completely forgetting that he was in the kids' room and not his smoking haven kitchen.

When we were cheering at the news of the two Ceauşescu's being caught while on the run they were experiencing already their 28th hour of captivity.

When they were taken to that military compound in Targoviste, they asked the commander, Colonel Kamenici, who he was taking orders from.

"With the situation in Bucharest, in my papers it is written that I shall take orders from General Gusa, the commander of chiefs of staff of the Romanian Army", he answered.

"From the one that I sent to Timişoara to clean up the city and couldn't do the job properly?" Ceauşescu replied.

"Then, from the new minister of defense, Nicolae Militaru", the commander said tentatively.

"Impossible", Ceauşescu answered. "Militaru is a KGB agent I personally fired from the Army. It must be someone else".

"From General Stănculescu", answered the commander, because Stănculescu, after organizing the repression in Timişoara was now organizing Ceauşescu's firing squad.

"Yes, you're right. Son, you are taking orders from General Stănculescu. That's your minister not Militaru. I made

Stănculescu the Army minister this morning", Ceauşescu had said, and he appeared to be happy about that fact. He was in good hands he thought, unlike his not yet senile wife who saw it coming. When they fled the building of the Central Committee one day before, she had spat on all the generals there. "Traitors! Traitors!" she called them and she was right. After 28 hours of being held captive, with armed guards at the door, she was, as we were, but with completely different feelings, waiting for something gruesome.

I was about to go down to the basement to fetch the wine my father sent me to get when I heard a loud knocking at the gate. Leaving the heavy glass decanter in the snow, I ran upstairs but only when I was inside the house did I say:

"Dad, someone's at the gate!"

He looked worried muttering:

"Must be Vasile. He is late as usual. Mom left word for him to come and get the Christmas fruitcakes"

He stood up and with deliberate movements started to walk to the door. I wanted to follow, but he asked me to stay behind. He was afraid, I could tell, and so was mom, but I didn't quite understand why. With Ceauşescu prisoner and awaiting trial we were already free, weren't we?

"Nuţa!" My father's half hysteric half nervous voice erupted from downstairs and we all rushed to see what was happening.

My mom's 29 year old half brother was drunk, I could tell without getting too close, but that didn't bother my dad who was trying to carry him inside.

As strange as it was, my dad was insisting to help Vasile to walk despite my uncle's protests. Only when they got really close did I understand why. Behind them was a trail of what could only be blood. Somehow Vasile had gotten injured, and we all rushed to help.

Clean towels were whipped out of the closet by my furious mother.

"How dare you come here drunk and in this shape?" "Do you think we have it easy here?" she went on.

Half crying, Vasile protested:

"No, you don't understand".

"What don't I understand? You are drunk, that's what I understand", she roared at him.

"Nuţa, Nuţa!", her brother cried using her nickname.

"I was there, I went to see the Revolution!" he said and my mother seemed to get even angrier. Surely an injury got while fighting was a lot worse than one got from falling on icy roads.

After Vasile was set on the armchair facing the blaring TV, from which the now victorious Iliescu acted as Ceauşescu's clone with nobody seeming to notice, we all saw that the blood in the snow and on our carpets was coming from his left boot.

Curious, I took a closer look. Something was wrong. I knew those boots as the previous winter they were my father's, but they didn't have a hole in them then. They did now.

My sister saw it, too, and she quickly went out to get some fresh air. I also was getting lightheaded, but still, as the young man of the house I had to stay to see what it was.

Blood was not a new sight for me. Only a couple of days before I had collected liters of it into a bucket from our slaughtered pig, but the source of the blood was new. Vasile, despite being the drunk that he was, was a nice uncle. He took me fishing many times and bought me candies when I gave him some of my father's wine. Not a very good deal for my father, I should say.

A handmade woollen sock was slid off his foot. Blood soaked. Then my mom carefully removed it and placed it in a basin she had somehow grabbed from the bathroom downstairs in no time at all.

Now you have all seen at least one Terminator movie. When the Governor of California was shot you could see the metal inside his human-like body. That was exactly what I saw that night. The bullet that made a hole in Vasile's boots was buried in his leg just above the ankle.

Strangely we were all calm. Very calm. Maybe that was because we could see the bullet, maybe because we could see that the blood flow wasn't as bad as we all thought. Maybe because we expected something much worse.

Before my mom could do anything to stop him Vasile pulled out his pocket knife and took the bullet out. The blood started to flow and my father took Vasile's hands while mother clean the wound with the only thing we ever used for cleaning wounds, 98% pure alcohol.

"Don't waste it!" Vasile said. "You should treat my insides with it."

He continued to be light-hearted. Drunk and funny, until he had a bandage and a new sock. Unfortunately we didn't have other boots to offer him so he had to wear the one with the hole in it, and he wore it for at least five years after that night.

His story was simple. He got my mom's message and was about to come for the fruitcake when a drunk friend of his asked him to go to Sibiu to see the Revolution. The story was that food shops were only selling alcohol because of the lack of food, had been vandalised by the angry mobs and inside there was still plenty of free brandy. They were lucky to catch the noon train and made their way into the revolution-torn city looking for booze. The stores were looted indeed, but there was nothing left in them. However, the people on the street involved in the Revolution had brandy with them and they shared, so he got drunk. He was running towards the train station when someone shot at him and he got under a car. And gunfire was hitting the car above him from time to time or every time he moved. And he got shot and ran and somehow nobody shot him in the back. And he took a train and there were people on the train but he was afraid to show them he was wounded. They were talking about terrorists. About how evil the terrorists were. Always posing as decent people. So he sat there for 45 minutes and bled in silence in his boots and got off in Avrig. He came to our house not on the roads but along the train tracks and then crossed gardens until he got on our street, unseen by suspicious people but heard by their dogs.

Somehow it all made sense. Vasile was a magnet for trouble. The last job he had lasted less than two hours. He crashed the bus he was supposed to drive. Lucky for him nobody was in it when he decorated a ravine with that Made in Romania Rocar bus, and even luckier for him my dad knew his boss and promised to cover the crash. That bus was the property of the people of Romania and destroying public property resulted in prison terms or in paying for life from your salary for the damaged property.

That stupid law was abolished only in the late 90's. In 1995 when I first got a job in a newspaper there was a sad looking cameraman working with Romanian TV, the same TV station that broadcast the Revolution, and that sad looking cameraman was working for nothing. His entire salary was taken to pay for a BETA camera that was stolen from him while filming something, somewhere.

So Vasile who was again jobless during the Revolution – as he was for the next twenty years – was not required to pay for the bus.

"You are a magnet for trouble!" my mother shouted while she was preparing two over-sized bags. One big jar with fried ribs in lard, two big fruitcakes, a bottle of wine, potatoes and other food for his kids. I was wondering if he could get home with the jar intact, drunk as he was and shot in his leg.

But as shot as he was he looked much better than the time he got in that duck incident.

That "duck incident" as my father called it, happened one year before. It was exactly December 23rd and Vasile, after taking a fruitcake, wine and pork ribs and meat came back to get a duck. We had ducks and chickens then and my mom said she was too tired to kill it for him and prepare it, so he should take it alive, as it was. And he did.

He really was a magnet for trouble. When he got home one of his neighbors was, club in hand, looking for thieves outside. That neighbor had been robbed of all five of his ducks that very evening so, when he saw Vasile in the dark carrying a live duck he started to club him without asking any questions, and he continued until Vasile was lying unconscious in the snow. That bastard didn't even apologize when he was told that he had actually clubbed an innocent person nor was he punished. He had friends in the Communist Militia. And Vasile was a jobless drunk anyway. At least his duck was returned, our duck, and his wife made him soup from it and his girls ate meat again. They weren't scared by their father's face which they were used to seeing swollen every now and then.

My father always said that Vasile's troubles where his mother's fault. My father's mother-in-law had raised her two daughters with an iron hand. When my mom was in a boarding school, from which she graduated as a worker, and would ask her for 100 lei, the same amount that Ceaușescu promised as a raise in his final public speech, she used to get a long letter with only 20 lei. "Do you happen to know how difficult it is to make 100 lei?" was the sentence that usually opened that letter.

Yes, my maternal grandmother lived a very poor life in her village of Lodroman, in Alba county. She was a trained nurse but after the war had to leave the hospital in Cluj, where she had a job. Her father was a chiabur, a winegrower. They were a wine-making family and quite wealthy. Until the communists took their fortune and wines. That was the reason why my grandfather, the one I never knew, died. My grandmother from Lodroman always tells me that I look so much like him, but mom cannot tell. Like me she has no memory of him. She was only two years old when, harassed by the new communist power, her father, a war hero, died of illness. Strange that my grandmother blames his illness on the Russians who kept him prisoner in Siberia for many years, not the fact that everything was taken from him before his first and only child was born.

So this grandmother that lived in Lodroman and had a hard life buried her second husband before she was forty and was thrown in the street by the in-laws. So she had to build a house by herself, while raising her three kids, and she did it with an iron hand, as I first said, but that iron hand always changed into feathers when it came to Vasile.

"It's all her fault", my father was muttering. He was talking about Vasile being married to Teodora.

I remember well how my grandmother from Lodroman came to live in Avrig. My mom was the first in her family to come to our town to work at the glass factory and she brought her sister and then brother along. Her sister married soon after my mom did and Vasile rented a room in town. So, for some reason his mother decided he had to marry and she came and rented a room, close to our house, for three long years and spent her time quilting and selling the clothes and hats that she made and going every day to church for the service.

She knew that Vasile had to get a religious wife and Teodora was a churchgoer. She really was. She was from Oltenia and was working at Marsa Mechanical where she shared a room in an ugly company dorm with her sister. Sunday was their only day off and they put on their best dresses and went to church.

There my grandmother from Lodroman would watch them and only after a year of watching those sisters every Sunday, she introduced herself to them. Then she gave them some cakes, and when they were acquainted enough she invited them for lunch.

Soon the place she invited them to wasn't her nearby rented room but our kitchen where Vasile was also invited and after lunch they would go to the Palace gardens or to see a movie.

I know that because I was a moviegoer too. We had Romanian movies but on weekends there where either Hollywood movies or Bollywood musicals. It's hard to tell which were more crowded. The small cinema hall in our town had seated 310 but always sold more than 1000 tickets. When I got lucky I used to share a seat with my sister. Otherwise, I sat on the stage two meters from the screen. That was how I first saw Superman. And Star Wars, 4 and 5.

Vasile and Teodora would share a seat and after they would buy an ice-cream from the ice-cream machine which had only two flavors, vanilla and cocoa. That's right, not chocolate, because chocolate wasn't used to make it, but cocoa ice-cream.

In less then 3 months they decided to marry and they got the standard one bedroom apartment from our communist country, and my parents bought them all the furniture and things they needed.

But Teodora wasn't the woman that my grandmother from Lodroman was looking for. Her cooking skills were poor and she didn't know how to keep a house. She had lived below the poverty line when she was young, always eating what was to be found in stores, not what they produced or made themselves. She was a true product of our communist government.

In 1989 we heard news that Ceaușescu wanted to make everybody eat in canteens and huge canteens were about to be constructed. In Bucharest they were almost ready. Resembling circus tents they were called the Hunger Circuses. Ceaușescu's plan was to forbid people from cooking and eating at home. Be that as it may, I have to acknowledge that his mad plan suited Teodora very well who didn't cook and didn't make Vasile happy.

He continued to drink and change jobs and my grandmother, after a failed attempt at moving in with them to teach Teodora how to keep a house and mend clothes for a husband left pissed off for Lodroman.

She eventually came back. In 1992 my grandmother became senile and she sometimes left home and wasn't able to find her way back. So my father went to Lodroman and came to an agreement with his mother-in-law so that she would come and live with us and watch over my grandmother. And she did, and watched over her, but never put much effort into the job. My mom was the one that cooked for the entire family, washed all our clothes, bathed my senile grandmother and, when she was confined to her bed without hope of recovery, slept in the same room with her. We were people, not animals and people had to pass away with their kin holding their hands and lighting candles for the soul to see the light of heaven and the way to the Holy Father, the Son, and the Holy Spirit.

As a communist to be, I used to say that I didn't believe in God! But it seems that the magnet for trouble was watched over by the Holy Trinity on that evening and he got home with the fruitcakes and jar of fried ribs in lard and the other food and wine we prepared for his family. But neither the Father, nor the Son, nor the Holy Spirit were working on that late evening in Bucharest.

Or at least they were only contemplating what people were doing with their free will.

The truth is that people don't quite understand what free will is. And they certainly didn't understand what freedom should be. Or, some of them did, but avoided setting the people free as much as possible.

The new Defense Minister, General Militaru was definitely from the latter category. Iliescu wanted terrorists and he was about to provide them. The whole country wanted the terrorists caught and he wanted to provide that, too, he wanted to serve.

Ceauşescu had stopped Militaru from serving eleven years before 1989. It was 1978 and Militaru was a three star general when he was pulled out of active duty and given a position in management in the Construction Industry Ministry - luckily for him.

He was lucky. Ceauşescu feared the Russians. Militaru's name came out in the Raven's file as a GRU agent. The GRU was the secret service of the Red Army, and this was the reason why Ceauşescu took the Second Army from Militaru's command and gave him that petty job in the construction industry. He would have been killed if Ceauşescu didn't fear the Soviet backlash, that's for sure.

Twenty years after 1989 I see the events more clearly. But on that night I was young and stupid, and open to being manipulated like the other 23 million Romanians.

It all started with a character that you don't know yet but you already hate. This man, because a man he was, was General Ion Hortopan. Only a couple of days before, when I was starting to smoke the pig, he was smoking the barricades around the Intercontinental Hotel in Bucharest. The soldiers that killed Jean Louis Calderon, the French journalist that would become a street name, were following his orders.

Maybe that was why he wanted to do something to stay afloat, maybe that was why Militaru decided to use him, I don't know, even now, twenty years later.

However, it all started when General Hortopan entered a meeting of the new power with the chief of USLA, the Romanian version of SWAT, and said loudly:

"Fighting has broken out outside Bucharest. Private-Major Popa has been captured. He was with USLA".

"I'm sure that Trosca is behind this!" replied the Romanian SWAT chief, General Ardelean. "Only he could be behind this."

Strangely enough, that name didn't ring a bell for anyone. How were they to know that Trosca was the man that took the Second Army from General Militaru in 1978?

As a counter-intelligence agent with the Second Army Trosca was the one that put Militaru on the Raven's List. Trosca was the one that conducted house searches at Militaru's home, Trosca was the one that called Militaru a traitor, and at that moment Trosca was the Major Chief of Staff of USLA.

It all looked like the events wouldn't go as planned, but that was only because Iliescu took his time while he made Militaru, officially, the Minster of Defense. Iliescu was tired, everybody was tired. But they had made it. They had taken control of the locomotive, as Brucan had put it, so they had to follow some bureaucratic procedures. For example when Iliescu signed the papers that started procedures for the Ceaușescus' trial one day before, he was officially only the head of the Technical Publishing House, but 24 hours later he was the head of FSN, the National Salvation Front, the iron grip that took Romania from Ceausecu and kept it away from the historical liberal, social democrat and christian democrat parties.

Not even a month later the FSN called on all workers to beat the shit out of those protesting the new communist-looking power, and they did it again when Iliescu and Roman asked the miners of Valea Jiului to beat up people who were pushing for reforms. The miners came and any intellectual-looking people they caught they beat, some they left with life-long injuries, some they simply killed. "Intellectual-looking" were the students, those they found in universities, in libraries, in bookstores, people wearing beards and glasses.

"We work, we don't think" was the miners' slogan and surely Iliescu thanked them for saving the Revolution, or more like his ass and power, or whatever.

But on that 23rd of December the miners were a card still to be played. The man of the day was Trosca.

Trosca was the one with the intelligence, with the information that, combined, would unveil who the people who climbed into Brucan's locomotive were. And that was the very reason Militaru called General Ardelean after receiving the ministry officialy from Iliescu, along with his 4th general star.

"Take 600 USLA troups and come to the ministry. There are snipers in the surrounding buildings. Come and take them out". His order was clear. So General Ardeleanu phoned the Romanian SWAT, his own troops and spoke with colonel Bleort.

"I understand, sir! Colonel Trosca is standing right here, sir!, Yes, sir!", was what Bleort yelled into the military phone, before giving the orders to Trosca.

On that night there were 647 USLA professional soldiers in Romania. 30 of them were guarding Embassies, 80 were sent to Sibiu to clear out the terrorists there, but Trosca didn't want to take all of the remaining 500 or so.

First he was suspicious. He knew who had given the orders. He knew that there were soldiers in the ministry that didn't need outside help for a sweep, he knew what had happened at Otopeni that morning.

But the order was clear, and he had to go. So he took 14 soldiers he could trust, boarded 3 ABI - laughable light armored military-grade Romanian-made Jeep-looking 4x4 ARO vehicles - and off he went, into the night.

Two years previously a Romanian made ARO with a Japanese made engine came in first in the World Famous Paris-Dakar endurance rally, but it was slow, and noisy and uncomfortable to drive. A car for shepherds, was how it was known and at school everybody made fun of those kids whose fathers had AROs.

This is why, even when I am told, 20 years after that night that one of those three ABIs broke down halfway to its destination, I'm not surprised.

Perhaps the Father, the Son and the Holy Spirit were doing their work that night. The five in it had to stay behind and their lives were spared.

But Trosca had to go on to defend his new Minister of Defence, the traitor that he had pulled out of the Army, General Militaru.

It was dark and when they got close to the new and huge ministry building, he started to believe that Militaru was right. Someone was attacking the building, but they weren't snipers. Coz what he heard was heavy fire, AKM's and heavier than those.

And then the Ministry came into view and then he knew he was right about Militaru back in '78, so he ordered his men to stop and they just watched what was going on, thinking.

After 10 minutes of watching he picked up his radio and called Bleort. He didn't have time to think that all words starting with BLE in Romanian had negative meanings. Like "bleg", which is weak, or "blenoragie" which was a sexually transmitted disease...

"Sir, allow me to report, sir!" he said.

"Yes", Bleort said eagerly.

"Here at the Ministry there is a motorcade of 7 or 8 Army TABs, two trucks full of army soldiers, two AROs and they have all been shooting their guns at the ministry for ten minutes and now they have stopped to reload."

"Whhhhaaaaat?" At the other side of the city, Bleort suddenly stood up. He was a spy, too, and he smelled treason.

"No way!" he yelled to his man.

"That's the truth!" replied Trosca.

"At the Ministry, you say?", Bleort went again, sweating...

"They have been shooting at the National Ministry of Defense and now they have stopped, roger that, sir."

"And now they've stopped?" Bleort asked nervously.

"Yes, they have, sir!", Trosca replied.

"Well, stop your vehicles by the last tank defending the Ministry and call us back so we can contact the ministry", ordered Bleort, with the feeling that that was the last order he would ever give Trosca.

"Roger that, sir", was the reply, and the two ABIs were already advancing until they stopped, as they were told, by a tank that had turned off its lights. Moments later everybody was shooting at them.

Like millions of Romanians, that night I was watching the Revolution live with my family. After so many years of seldom being used, the TV had become the most important member of our family. Crying or shouting the TV was like a baby that had to be watched 24 hours a day.

When one of us went downstairs to take a shower or use the toilet or to get a piece of fruitcake, he or she would ask, for the first time in Romania's history, "what happened while I was away?" But we were told only the things that we were allowed to watch, not everything.

We were told that the Army had become a target of the terrorists. After the bloody repression that the Army had taken part in in Timişoara and Bucharest, the Army was now fighting for the people and not against them. But we never imagined that the Army was fighting the Army. There weren't enough dead bodies. Enough for who? Even now I wish I knew for sure...

Three survivors of that night are still looking for the same answer.

Back in 1989 inside their ABI two men were killed instantly by heavy machine guns. Those bullets 20 or so centimeters long left one of them without the lower part of his face. The hole left, opened widely to expose the throat and the terror in his eyes replaced the scream that would come only as a spray of blood from his lungs. And it stayed open as the others started to hide behind his body, on the floor of that ABI.

"They're shooting at us!" Trosca yelled in the radio. The shooting continued and there was no response. After another minute, there were 4 dead and another six hiding for their lives inside or under the ABIs. Nobody dared to move. They knew they would be seen. The soldiers shooting at them were on higher ground...

"Trosca, report. Are you still there?"

The calm voice of Colonel Bleort came from the heavy radio Trosca was holding.

"Yes, sir! We have four casualties. Sir! What's happening?"

I had the ministry on the phone. They said you need to confirm you're Trosca and his men and not terrorists. Shoot three florescent green flares into the sky! Three! You get that? They will respond with more flares and then you'll be safe!"

"Roger, sir!".

Trosca didn't need to give the order because his men had heard the conversation. Suddenly there was silence. The army soldiers shooting at them stopped. Three similar florescent green flares went up in the black winter sky. The same flares were shot by officers on New Year's Eve with "borrowed" pistols, since the communist government didn't organize firework displays. They had to celebrate with their families somehow.

Then the flares started to come down. Lower, lower and Trosca and his remaining 5 men looked towards the positions near the ministry. There was complete silence. Only their heartbeats and the blood dripping from the two ABIs made any sound.

Three bangs, and similar flares started to climb into the sky above the menacing TAB's. They were happy. Maybe happier than they were on New Year's.

Two of them got to their feet and started to wave.

Boom, boom, boom, boom.

The nearest TAB's heavy machine gun ripped huge holes through their bodies. Other smaller guns started to rattle and the four survivors responded with fire. Only three of them saw morning alive. Trosca was the last to die that night and after Bleort got the news and screamed again on the phone at someone inside the Ministry, the shooting stopped and didn't start again.

At that time I was already asleep, despite the fact that my father stayed to watch the revolution from the same armchair where we put Vasile when we mended his gunshot wound. He feared the communists would gain control again. The news was that after they had attacked the Airport in the morning they attacked the Ministry of Defense and were still attacking it as the news came in. A civil war would be even worse than the Russians he thought, before falling asleep where he sat.

He didn't realize that everything was a joke, a sinister joke. The communists already had taken over, the day before, just after Ceaușescu fled in his white helicopter. Iliescu and his band were about to plunge the country into despair. The whole wave of sympathy that Romania received from Europe was about to be washed away by the new power that wanted power more than they wanted prosperity and democracy for the people.

The terrorists that were attacking the Minsitry of Defense were not terrorists but USLA soldiers. The elite troups called to defend the building. Maybe they were people my father served with in the Alpen Corps, from which USLA professionals were recruited, maybe, nobody knows.

Only twenty years later did people start to speak about that night, and they say that Bleort called the ministry four times. The first time to tell them that Trosca and 14 of his men were going to come to help with the terrorist sweep. The second time he called to ask them to cease fire. The third time to say he would fuck them all because they were just a bunch of criminals and, the last time to say the same thing, and something more because he had learned that Trosca had been killed.

How was that possible? Only General Militaru knew. He was in a room full of officers when he was told that his people had opened fire on Trosca, but he preferred to retreat to his office to speak on the phone. He was alone when he set everything up, when he gave the orders, and his orders were followed as they were supposed to be. He was the Minister of Defense, not just some ass working on construction projects for Ceaușescu.

"Every last one" must have been his order, but my father had no idea, his kids, me and my sister, were innocently sleeping beside him on our lined up beds, his wife in the main bedroom and it was already the 24th of December, Christmas Eve that we could celebrate properly, the day of joy, the birth of Christ.

4. DECEMBER 24ᵀᴴ

When I worked as a journalist I sometimes saw raw footage from war-torn African countries and I always felt sick after seeing people set ablaze alive, or people throwing enemies alive on bonfires and part of me believed that such acts of cruelty could never happen in a country like Romania.

Why are people so cruel to each other? I couldn't understand it. But the truth is that people can stoop lower than animals. We are the scum of the earth.

The story, the real story, of course, is that when people living close to the Ministry of Defense woke up on the morning of the 24th they took from their fruitcakes and from their sweets and food and went to give it to the soldiers defending the Revolution.

"Merry Christmas!"

"Merry Christmas, to you too!"

The fruitcakes changed hands, food changed hands, some soldiers got handmade woollen sweaters to wear under their military jackets and coats. But this Merry Christmas wishing crowd looked down the street and saw it paved with bullets and used cases. All kinds of calibers. Seven bodies were lying in and around two ARO looking military cars.

A man started to run and used his foot to hit a body in the head. The head, like a real football, detached and rolled over to the joy of those watching. That head had belonged until less than 8 hours before to a hero, Colonel Trosca, the very man that took the Second Army from General Militaru back in 1978.

A football game to play on Christmas Eve! And what a funny football game it was. That head that rolled from one to another only to be hit again symbolized Ceaușescu and their hardship and they took revenge for the days without meat and heat, for the cheap beer and fake coffee.

They would have played that game all day long but someone had the idea of torching the bodies, and they did it with some gas they took from one of the ABI tanks.

Torched, Trosca's head was placed on the spare wheel mounted on an ABI's hood. Someone put a cigarette in its charred lips and almost everybody, before returning to their peaceful homes for their peaceful Christmas Eve, for carols and fruitcake and all those little things that turn a normal day into the most perfect Christmas Eve, spat on that head.

"Merry Christmas!" they shouted to the soldiers defending the Ministry building, before leaving, and, they said "Merry Christmas" again on December 25th in the morning, when they came to give the soldiers more fruitcake and food, and the bodies were still scattered on the ground, and Colonel Trosca's head was still there with that cigarette in its charred lips mounted on the car, and we were the people that I didn't believe capable of the cruelties that I was seeing in raw footage from places like Africa.

I woke up happy.

Christmas Eve was by far, the best day of the year.

As usual, I was already alone in my room. My sister was already up and her bed was made up neatly. I did mine quickly and then I opened the bottom drawer of a bookshelf and I took out the vacuum cleaner.

My parents' room was first, ours came second and, lastly I did the hallway. Only after finishing did I want to go downstairs. I was placing the vacuum cleaner back in its box when my mom and my sister entered the room holding cleaning cloths and buckets of hot water. They had to dust everything and use wet brushes to brush the Persian carpet we had in our parents' room.

After saying good morning I was already making my escape before my mom invented another chore for me.

"Your breakfast is on the table under that white cloth!", my mom said to my back, but I was thinking "Fruitcake, fruitcake, fruitcake, milk".

And fruitcake it was!

Now that was a beautiful morning. I put the home made butter and jam back in the pantry and returned the bread to the cupboard and started to eat the three kinds of fruitcake that we made a day earlier and drink cold milk. I don't know why my mom always wanted us to drink the milk hot, but with her upstairs I could have it my way. Cold, in a tall glass. That day's particular glass had a red Santa painted on it and in white, close to the top was written in English: "Merry Christmas, Florin!". It was my favorite.

I got the glass from my mom's glass factory the same year my grandfather died . The workers' union made Christmas bags for every child whose parents worked there. Usually sweets, but on that particular year they were allowed by the factory's director to produce personalized glasses for all the kids. The message on the glasses had to be in English. They were not allowed to write "Merry Christmas!" in Romanian, and the red Santa wasn't supposed to come before New Year's Eve.

It surely sounds insane, but the communist government promoted a secular Santa despite the fact that in the western world Santa was already secular!

A Christian Father Christmas, as we used to call him, wasn't supposed to wear a red coat, live at the North Pole and have his sled pulled by a red-nosed Rudolph & Co. The real Father Christmas was just an idea. He used to live in Heaven and he was the husband of the woman that allowed the Holy Virgin Mary to give birth to Jesus in the stable. We were told that he got so mad that his wife allowed strangers close to their animals that he cut off both her hands, as any other reasonable and sane Middle Eastern man would have done.

But God saw what he had done and sent the Holy Spirit to fix the woman's hands and her hands jumped from the ground and glued themselves back to the woman's battered arms, the same way the liquid metal Terminator did with its own hands. So Father Christmas saw the will of God and after King Herod killed all children younger than two he sold all his possessions and bought food to feed the Jewish kids in his town. And then he died of hunger himself because, having sold everything, death was his only possible fate. He got to go to Heaven and from there sometimes, not always and not to all kids, he would present kids with gifts, or, warm the hearts of adults causing them to buy gifts for kids.

See what I'm saying? Our Father Christmas had nothing to do with Santa. Santa was as secular as Father Frost on New Year's Eve. Father Frost was the name of the communist Santa.

Anyway, the workers' union managed every year to distribute their bags on December 24th, and even now in Romania, after so many years, Santa comes on Christmas Eve, rather than Christmas Day from the North Pole or wherever he comes from.

Who cares? Santa is secular anyway.

But on that particular 24th of December, I was waiting for Father Christmas. The real one. Only Father Christmas could warm all hearts and turn evil people into good folk. And Father Christmas was real. Not in the way Santa is believed to be in the western world with the idiots from NORAD tracking his sled.

Father Christmas was real because he warmed the communist hearts and made them put oranges and bananas in stores before Christmas, and not after it, in January, or something. He was real because the God-hating communists sold Christmas ornaments in communist stores, beautiful handmade and hand-painted Christmas globes. Because workers were sent to cut Christmas trees from Ceaușescu's forests and people could buy them to decorate their homes for Christmas and not only New Year's Eve.

I knew that whatever Christmas presents we got they were from our parents, but Father Christmas definitely played his role when my mom and dad could save money for presents.

I emptied my "Merry Christmas, Florin!" glass and took a kitchen knife and went outside. The Christmas tree was standing in the snow in the same spot Finul Moisică had left it the day before. I took it and hit it against the clean ground twice. The snow at its bottom fell off. Then I started to cut the bottom off so that it would fit in our homemade Christmas tree stand.

The stand had a 15cm pipe right in the middle of it and it was into that pipe I had to fit and fix the Christmas Tree. My father said that when a friend of his made us that stand we had no bigger pipe, and that was the reason I or my father had to work for half an hour or so every year outside chopping at the Christmas tree so it would fit in that pipe.

We heard many stories of Christmas trees that fell down and entire households were lost in the resulting fires. Yes, that's right. Back then all ornaments were made from very thin painted glass and we could place real candles on the Christmas tree, taking care not to place them below upper branches, and we used to light those candles and tell Christmas stories in their dim but beautiful light.

How beautiful it was. But still, I had to chop and chop until my Christmas tree was just a little bit thicker than its stand. And I was sweating hard to get it done that year.

As usual the tree was taller than it needed to be. Our ceiling was 3m high, but that Christmas tree was also 3m high so I had to cut about 3cm off it to allow for the top decoration and stand.

Furious hacking took the bottom off in minutes. But that was only the beginning. The knife was sharp enough to cut the young tree, but I had to hold the tree upright all the time, so as not to damage its branches. The whole process became more and more difficult.

Think I had protective gloves? Think again. Communist Romania wasn't a consumer society and we had no such gloves. Even people working in industry with hot iron sometimes had to work with bare hands, and it's amazing what people can learn to endure in time. But I didn't have tough hands and as a fourteen year old my skin was still like a child's. The cold tree started to hurt my fingers as it sucked the heat out of them, long before I was tired from cutting. But I couldn't stop. Not then. I couldn't take a break, I couldn't cry for help. The bottom of the tree was getting thinner and thinner so I had to continue for the joy of that day.

My dad would be so proud. It used to be his job and while I was standing beside him in the cold, in the years of my childhood, it seemed a very easy job to do. Cut. Turn. Cut. Turn. And cut again. But the job wasn't easy. Even the task of keeping the tree up was a complicated one. But perseverance was the key so I continued until I had it done.

Stretching my back, 40 minutes after I had started, I set the tree standing in the snow and I went inside for a hot cocoa and the stand I had cleaned.

Cocoa was my favorite drink that time of year. On rainy days too. I always made it myself, not trusting my mom to do it right. Three tablespoons of Dutch cocoa, three tablespoons of sugar and, because it was so cold outside, an egg yolk. Then came the frenetic mixing while the milk was being heated on the hub. The secret of a tasty drink was to pour the milk into the mug little by little and as you mixed it in.

And there I was, with a mug of hot cocoa at the window, looking outside at the snow. That morning my mom must have made the willow fire. Smoke had started to fill the smokehouse. The snow on its roof was already butter yellow and I hoped it would melt in the next couple of days. A butter yellow roof wasn't a sight that suited Christmas.

My father wasn't home and I supposed that he was at the town hall, in the middle of our town's own revolution. With the communist mayor gone and the communist party office completely vandalized there wasn't so much to do there. Some soldiers from the Military Unit guarding the Marsa Mecanichal had been brought in to help defend the building in case of a terrorist attack, but with Ceaușescu prisoner that was unlikely to happen.

My hands were already hot when I finished the hot cocoa drink. We always had first class cocoa powder from the Netherlands or China, so my mornings were always perfect. That Seagull cocoa powder we got in those big orange cans from Shanghai was especially delicious. But we weren't always lucky enough to find it every time so we had to buy the lower quality Dutch cocoa.

I couldn't have known that day that freedom would, in a matter of only a couple of months, bring to our stores tons of instant cocoa drinks made by Nestle which compared in taste with the cocoa that I made that day, like tap water in New Delhi compares to Evian.

Yes, capitalism wasn't as delicious as we imagined it.

"What's this? Chicken or fish?" was a question that I never asked before we were "free". Chickens during communist times would take more than a year to grow big enough to eat. And they tasted like chicken. Fish tasted like fish. Pork tasted like pork not like salted something or other. The food produced in Romanian farms was all organic, the word steroids hadn't yet entered the Romanian vocabularly and antibiotics were just for very sick people not for the birds, fish and mammals in our food chain.

I took the cleaned and polished Christmas tree stand outside. The front yard was the best spot to fix the tree into it, and not in our parents' room, where the tree traditionally stood.

I placed the support on a patch of clean icy ground, where it was unlikely to get dirty, and I brought the tree over to it. I only had one go at getting it set in the stand right.

I intentionally left the end of the tree a little bit larger than the pipe in which I was going to set it, so when in, it would stay in. Carefully I placed the tree right over the dark pipe and then I forced it down into it with an almost perfect hit. When I lifted the tree again in the air the stand lifted, too, so I hit it once again, with all my strength. I was done.

Satisfied I took the tree upstairs. When I entered the hallway my mom was there on the phone.

"Why don't you go to the doctor?" she was asking in a pissed off tone. "Ceauşescu has been caught, you are safe - the police won't ask questions about how you got wounded".

I realized that she was on the phone with Vasile. Later I learned that he called her to tell her he needed something stronger than wine. His leg had doubled in size over night and brandy was the best painkiller he could think of.

His wife Teodora was about to arrive to fetch some bottles.

My mom spoke in a very angry tone.

"If you don't promise me you'll go to the doctor or ask the doctor to come and see you, I won't give her any brandy, do you hear me?"

My mom ended up giving him the brandy. He promised to go for medical treatment, but it was February 1991 before we learned that he hadn't gone. He poured the brandy on the wound and in his stomach, too, and got better before New Year's Eve. However, in the long run that choice was a very poor one.

Iliescu wanted very good servants when he battled the liberals and christian democrats for power, so his government started to give gifts to the revolutionaries.

There were commissions formed and if people could prove they were involved in the events or got wounded they would receive a fortune.

Vasile couldn't receive anything. He was shot but got no award. So he missed out on the apartment that others got, the 500 square meters of land inside a town or 10,000 square meters outside towns, tax exemption for life on a piece of real estate of his choice, among other benefits.

Others were not even shot and hit the jackpot. Like the mother-in-law of the 2009 Presidential Candidate, Mr. Geoana. She was, like many in the television station, not a victim but a beneficiary of the communist regime. So after the Revolution she claimed that she had dropped a box on her right leg and got injured. And she hit the jackpot. And 20 years later still claims that that leg hurts, but now she points to the other leg, or at least that's what we read in the newspapers.

Mr. Geoana, too, was involved in the Revolution. His father, the famous Securitate General Geoana introduced him to Iliescu. "This is my son, Mr. President! Our country needs young people like him", he said and left the young Geoana with him.

I met him in the summer of 1996. My boss held a party for him when he was appointed Romania's Ambassador to the United States. Years later Iliescu got sick of him and called him "the dumb one", and that name stuck with Geoana so well that if you search for "prostanac" you can see that he ranks number one in both Google and Yahoo.

Anyway, Romania was too poor to award all those who really fought in the Revolution with houses and land. Or got injured when looking for booze, like Vasile.

As my mom banged down the phone Teodora was already opening the gate.

It was the 24th, Christmas Eve and we had to leave the door open for the carol singers.

Teodora had the kids with her, three very beautiful little girls and they sang. My mom instantly warmed when she saw them. So she invited them inside and gave them sweets and money. Then asked their mother to not let their father to take the money from the girls. He used to. Over the years we gave them a slide, a bicycle...and he traded all their toys for brandy.

He even traded his fridge for alcohol but that particular trade was not a good one at all, despite the fact that he got almost one month's supply of it.

"He traded his fridge for pufoaică brandy", shouted my father one day after he came home from work.

And the rest of us replied together "Wwwhhhaaaaaaaatttttt????"

You'd go "What?", too, if you knew what pufoaică brandy was.

So, here's the question: have you ever seen pictures of Russian soldiers or Russian workers in winter? If the answer is yes, then you probably know that the Romanian name of what they were wearing is "pufoaică".

The story goes that Russian winter clothes, when introduced into a common latrine, start fermenting when in contact with urine and feces and where there is fermentation there is alcohol too. Nobody knows who it was who dared to boil and then distill this fermenting sewage but someone must have because cheap alcohol lovers got to drink it.

"They probably produce it industrially", my father once said, obviously full of admiration for the ingenuity of the people who made booze from clothes and shit.

Those were the times we were living in! And what times they were! It's interesting to think back and realize that I never ever heard of people getting sick after drinking that pufoaică brandy. It seems that the only downside to it was the awful smell. But who we are to judge them? Japanese potato brandy doesn't smell good either and some bottles cost more then 100 dollars each.

But over the following years of economic downturn when people started to lose their jobs and inflation skyrocketed with prices going up almost daily, other Romanians got smart and added chicken poo mixed with the paste obtained from water melted arc welding sticks to the pufoaică brandy recipe. And that got even more alcohol out of it. Some drinkers forever ruined their health while others were faster and simply died.

Newspapers reported on pufoaică brandy but their articles were to sell papers not to point out to the government the plight of its population.

"Must have been the heavy metals in those welding sticks" was the popular conclusion given at funerals.

"He shouldn't have drunk that pufoaică brandy. Matrafox is much more safer", was another popular comment.

Now, if you are confused and don't know what matrafox is, I can tell you that it is something that is very easy to make. Just take an ounce of any alcohol based aftershave that you have in your house, pour it into a two liter plastic bottle, add the contents of a peppermint toothpaste tube, some sugar, fill with water and shake. And shake. And wait for a day or two and then you can label the bottle "Matrafox". It's still a popular drink in Romanian prisons. It gives the euphoria that real booze gives and the headaches the following day too. Or maybe just the headaches, I don't know for sure, since I didn't have the guts to taste my homemade Matrafox.

But again, those were the times. People were made poor by Iliescu and his men, people became desperate.

But the bright side of those times was the beautiful silver plated Christmas Tree in my parents' room.

My mom and my sister were looking at it and turned it around to find the best side that would face the door. Our house was already super clean and we were eager to start covering the tree with our glass decorations. The house was so warm. As usual in winter when the gas pressure dropped we supplemented the gas with firewood, twice a day, in the morning and before going to bed. The defrosting tree started to spread its perfume throughout the house.

That was the moment I was waiting for all year. The real smell of Christmas.

"If we'd had oranges it would have smelled even better", said my sister, reading my mind.

"I'm sure next year we'll have plenty", my mom said as she left to start cooking and baking.

She was as usual, right. In less than one year oranges were as common as apples and we didn't put them under the Christmas tree anymore. Strange as it was, our last real Christmas was in 1989. It died right there with the two Ceaușescus and nobody cared to notice.

Things turned so commercial afterwards. People bought plastic Christmas trees and pine scented air fresheners to replace the real thing, candles were forgotten and replaced with Made in China Christmas lights, candies were no longer hung on the tree and obese kids do not worship them since they fed themselves on Swiss made chocolate bars every day.

Maybe it's wrong to complain like this, but as a carol singer you now are more likely be greeted with the same brands of Christmas cookies that everybody has, on the traditional rounds on the 24th, than the carefully homemade fruitcakes and cornulete.

I was still admiring our beautiful tree, before opening the boxes with the decorations, when my mom called me from downstairs. Teodora was about to leave and I had to cut the pine branches off the tree bottom for she was to take them home with her.

I had completely forgotten that the tree was always the same height year after year for the same reason. Vasile's family didn't have a tree so we would give them three branches they would hang and decorate in their living room. One branch was for Uncle Lulu who used to buy a tree for his living room, but a small one, and he always wanted a branch to decorate his kitchen, the place where almost all visitors were invited.

"Cut all four of them, Teodora will give one to Anişoara", said my mom.

"Isn't it too dangerous to go home that way?" I asked , thinking about the town center where the revolution was taking place, but my mom replied:

"They came that way, and apart some half burned piles of books and smashed windows everything is back to normal".

I didn't say anything but I wondered why nobody cared to lift the curfew on me and my sister since everything was "back to normal", but I didn't realize at that time that "normal" was just the fact that our town was peaceful. Nothing more, nothing less. That "normal" didn't have a predictable future. The terrorists were still battling with the Revolution in Bucharest and Sibiu, the two Ceauşescus were caught and awaiting trial, their kids were imprisoned and their dogs were, to general applause, clubbed to death. What was next nobody knew, nobody dared to imagine. People were still afraid.

After you are afraid for so long it's very difficult not to be afraid anymore. We were like caged animals that wouldn't leave their open cage. Brucan was aware of this simple fact, and so was Iliescu, but we weren't and that's why we accepted the new power made by people that served Ceausescu and his despotic regime and that's why we rejected the unknown, the Liberals and Christian Democrats.

The four branches came off that 30cm long tree end and my mom wired three of them together. They were beautiful. I wished I had such long branches last year instead of the plastic tree I bought in Japan for my kids. These are the times we live in now...

Back upstairs with my sister, after Teodora had left with her fairytale little girls, the brandy for her shot and drunk husband and the Christmas tree branches, we started to decorate our tree. First we attached the biggest glass ornaments, then smaller ones until the tree looked like it was supposed to look. Only then did we add the candies wrapped in colored paper and finally the candles.

The candle business was a delicate job, we had to carefully put them in place making sure they would burn without setting the tree and our house ablaze. But even that job couldn't compare with the placing of the tree topper.

Usually my dad did it, but that year I had decided I was man enough to do the job myself. However, a chair to climb on was not high enough, and even a table was still short. Therefore it had to be a table, a chair and me on top of that.

Felicia was already starting to panic and in her usual way threatened me in a loud voice that she would call mom. But she didn't. She wasn't a snitch, so she had to stay and help.

I got a table close to the tree and put a chair on it, close to the edge facing the tree. Then I carefully climbed on the table, and from the table on to the chair.

I was afraid of heights. My knees were trembling when I lowered my hand to take the tree topper handed to me by Felicia.

It was a nice topper. It looked like a potato being screwed by a huge carrot - in one end, out the other. My father always laughed and called it a "dick", and I didn't understand what it meant, but our secular communist society had earlier rejected all Christian symbols and transformed the star-shaped Christmas Tree toppers into carrot screwed potatoes. Communism was about to end and I was about to find out that we had been missing a star on the top of our tree. But again, I didn't know all that. My mind was glued to only my careful movements, the way

I stood up and reached with my left hand to the tree top while my right hand was holding the topper tighter than it should. My body was tense when, holding my breath, I put the topper in place.

At that very moment many things happened at once. First my left hand released the tree. The tree snapped back and I thought it was going to fall down so I tried to reach back to hold it, but then I lost my fragile balance. The chair slipped off the table, my feet still on it, so I did the only thing I could do, I pushed it by suddenly straightening my knees so it fell with a loud crash on the floor while I was flattened, face down on the table.

Felicia was shouting, pointing at some scattered glass decorations on the blood red carpet, but the tree was still standing so I closed my eyes and tried to understand something above the rush of adrenaline that suddenly flowed in my body.

No matter how big the adrenaline kick that I got falling down was, it was nothing compared with the one that Colonel Kamenici was experiencing at that very moment.

He was the commander of the military unit to which the Ceauşescus were brought on the 22nd, but at that moment he wanted to be anything but the man in charge.

He was biting his nails, turning in his head, over and over again, the words of General Voinea, the head of the First Army.

"You can, Colonel, can't you?...Understand that you are finished? It's you or Ceauşescu. Only one of you will survive this Revolution. Remember, it's you or him".

That was the night of December 22nd, and he wasn't stupid. So he called General Stănculescu and asked for more troops to guard the dictatorial couple, but he was denied.

"Then, if we are attacked and outnumbered, be sure, my General, we won't hand over the Ceauşescus alive", he said bombastically, like he was the main character in an American movie. But the answer that he got was not the one that he expected:

"That's a good plan. When you hand them over be sure they are dead".

That was the reason he was biting what was left of his nails. He was watching the TV like any other Romanian at the time and saw that the same people that ordered Ceuasescu dead on the 22nd, pretended for more than a day that they were still pursuing Romania's president and battling his terrorists. Was it all fake? Perhaps, but he knew it was him or Ceaușescu, so he had to get Ceaușescu killed as soon as possible.

Only it was something quite difficult to do. He was still nervous about the missed opportunity from the previous day. Somebody called their unit and said that in 30 minutes they would be under heavy air attack so he turned to two majors he had in his commanding room and barked:

"Mares, you go and execute Ceaușescu! Tecu, you execute Elena! Now!", and they went and everybody was waiting. They were listening for aircraft noise, but he was listening for shots, but those shots never came.

It turned out that his majors, Ion Mares and Ion Tecu, were waiting for the bombing to start before executing his order, so, as the bombing never started, they refused to obey. "It's you or him". Those words were ringing in his head, louder and louder. There had to be something else, he thought, something that would get him out of this unscathed.

I was getting down from the table while my sister was gathering the shattered glass globes on a piece of paper. She was using a real duck wing for the job, instead of a miniature broom. We always kept the duck wings for they were good for dusting and sweeping furniture, floors and carpets.

In the next room, our room, the TV set came to life. After switching it on it always took five minutes to start blasting out images and sounds. It had no transistors inside, only lamps, the same technology that was used in the western world in 40's and early 50's.

The revolution was continuing, it seemed. The terrorists were still attacking our dear soldiers and there were reports that they wanted to set Ceaușescu free.

While Felicia was finishing collecting the broken glass, I took a candy from the tree, unwrapped it and hung it up again, empty, on the same spot, and then I put the table and the chair back in their place.

We were done, and that tree was simply too beautiful. My father told me that Finul Moisică climbed full grown pines to cut off their tops for us and his family. Finul Moisică said the tops of full grown trees looked much better than young trees and the forest would stay intact. I didn't care what part of the tree we had there, an entire one, or just a top. All I cared was that the tree looked beautiful.

I was still admiring our work when I heard a car stopping at our gate. I took a look from the window and I froze. It was a military car. If I had looked better I would have seen that it was an ABI, but all I saw was a young soldier behind the wheel.

With my heart pumping even more adrenaline than a few minutes before when I almost broke some bones, I started to run outside. I had to put myself between that soldier and my family if they had murderous intentions. I had to.

I was very close to the gate when the handle went down and it opened wide. The Colonel was there and behind him was my smiling father.

"Boy, you should eat more, you're thinner than the last time I saw you", said The Colonel in his usual happy voice.

"Tell Nuţa we are here, and send her upstairs with food and wine", ordered my father while he was showing The Colonel upstairs.

That was a first. My father would usually receive his guests in the kitchen, where they would eat, drink and smoke until the food, and the cigarettes ran out. The wine never ran out. We made a few hundred liters every year.

I said to my mom in a hurry what dad wanted and rushed upstairs to listen to The Colonel. He was always telling interesting stories and I really wanted to be like him in the future. At 18 I was supposed to go to the Army and I wanted to be in the paratroops. I was fascinated by planes and ships but I never had the chance to see a plane, except those flying at high altitude above us, or a warship. But as a paratrooper I would be around planes all day long and I would not work in the fields or on construction sites as the military usually did. Dreams. I had so many.

The Colonel came to us because he was a man with a mission. He came to inspect my father but as people were going home for Christmas Eve, from the town hall, he wanted to go to a warm place, too, and listen to carols and eat and have some wine. So there he was, and my father was more than happy to have him as a guest, despite the fact that on Christmas Eve we usually had people coming and going, not staying with us for more than 30 minutes.

That year was definitely special. My mom felt it, too, when she entered with food and wine. The kids' room, the one with the TV set, was already filling up with smoke.

"Hey, you know it's not allowed to smoke here", my mom said, only half angry. "The walls will get dirty", she pointed, forgetting somehow me and Felicia.

"Doesn't matter. As soon as it gets warm we will have Sandu the house painter, here, to refresh the entire house", happily replied my father.

He was talking sense. Every second year we had Sandu the house painter, repaint our house inside, and every 6 years we had him do his magic outside too. Along with Mr. Bara, the tailor, he was self-employed. We liked him but we couldn't get close because he belonged to a different church. They celebrated the sabbath on Saturday, and that was the main reason Sandu refused to take a regular job and started to paint houses. Before 1989 only Sunday was a holiday, Saturday being a half day for workers. Another reason was that Sandu's religion asked him to be a strict vegan. He couldn't eat meat, fish, eggs or dairy products, so we couldn't invite him to eat with us on Sundays, the day we usually had guests. Sunday was a day we had to celebrate by eating our best food. We could be strict vegetarians from Monday to Saturday, but Sunday was different.

I had a classmate in the same church. I remember how our teacher, Mr. Napeu, once tried to make him eat salami, and how Silviu refused and battled to keep his mouth closed as the rest of us, rather than pity, envied him. We almost never saw salami, but that's another story. I also remember how my grandfather said he didn't like the vegans' extremism pointing out that "None of them lived to more than 50 years old. You can go and check their section in the cemetery. They all die young".

But the future was something we could not anticipate, especially the economic crisis and the inflation. So Sandu the painter wasn't called when it became warm, and, as a matter of fact, he never set foot inside our house again. Since 1989 we have painted our house only twice. First when my sister married in 1997 and last when I married in 2004, and every time it was my new brother-in-law who painted it, helped by his friend Viorel, that very nice gipsy boy who shared his first name with my father.

The Colonel was talking about terrorists and also about his suspicion that the terrorists didn't exist.

"I was in Sibiu today and I can tell you something. Nobody is shooting at Army positions, but the Army is shooting at everyone else. Everybody is paranoid and they are always saying on the TV that soldiers should fire without waiting for orders", he said then rushed to empty his wine glass.

"Good wine, you have here, Grancea", he said using my father's last name. "Have some taken to my ABI outside to those soldiers waiting", he asked me after he helped himself to another glass.

Curious, I went out and took from the basement an already filled one liter bottle and went outside to the ABI. The soldiers were inside but the engine was off. I could see they were cold. Before I reached the car, the driver rolled down the window and said:

"You're only bringing one bottle? Can't you see there are two of us?" so I handed that bottle to him and rushed in to get another one. They were right. Only one bottle on Christmas Eve for two people wasn't enough.

Back in my smoke-filled room The Colonel, now with a very red face asked me looking into my eyes:

"Son, you are free now. Ceauşescu is gone and he'll never come back. I'm sure his hours are numbered. So tell me, what do you want from this freedom? I wonder, because you are young and you must want different things than we, older people, want".

First I didn't know what to say. But because I was a top student and always immediately answered all questions put to me, I said without thinking:

"Shoes, new shoes".

My father pretended that he didn't hear my answer and so did The Colonel. They continued to watch the TV, to hear the messages that the new power was disseminating. They continued to drink their wine.

Ashamed by my answer, I excused myself and left, and once out I started to cry and the tears fell on my shoes, or should I say on the shoes that I was wearing because that weren't mine.

Almost a year before I'd had to buy new shoes. But because I was growing so fast I couldn't find any. In the shoe stores, in the adult section, the smallest I could find was the European size 40 and I needed 36. In the kids' section the biggest shoes were size 35. Too small to fit my growing feet.

I usually shopped with my family. Never alone. So we went every Saturday evening to a shoe store, in Avrig or in Sibiu to find shoes, but with no success. Finally, exasperated, my mom gave me 100 lei, the same amount that Ceaușescu promised as a pay raise in his last speech, and said:

Florin, you are a big boy now, go to the shoe store every day after you finish school and you'll get lucky. If you go on the day they receive new merchandise in the store, I'm sure you'll be able to find something your size".

And I went to buy shoes almost every day. And I kept that bank note of 100 lei in my pocket until its color faded and the paper looked worn out. Only two months after did I have the chance to use it. In Sibiu, from the communist version of a department store I bought, in the women's section, a ridiculous looking azure blue pair of shoes. Size 36, and I paid 60 lei for them . I wanted to buy a size 37, and the store clerk, a nice old lady advised me to wait another couple of months until the store received new supplies, but I could not wait anymore. The shoes I was wearing were so used and full of holes that I looked like a beggar the communist country was showing to us in pictures when they wanted to tell us about how people lived in America. I was 14 and I was in love with Adriana, a classmate, not that she was aware, but still.

So I put on my new azure blue and ridiculous looking women's shoes and walked away from the store, with my old shoes in a plastic bag. Those shoes would be repaired and used for gardening by my mother. That was the way it was. We never really threw anything away, not unless they were completely destroyed and could not possibly be used.

Anyway, my women's shoes lasted less than I expected. In less than one month my feet were already too big for them so I was sweating with fear every morning when I put them on. Pain. Blood. Pain. Terrible pain. Every step was a nightmare and I was doing it to myself. Nobody was forcing it on me. That was sick. That was how communism felt for me and that is, right now, my strongest memory of those days.

I used to hide my wounded feet, but one day my mom saw my bloody socks and cried out and I had to take my shoes off and she was saying she was sorry and that she loved me, and she was crying and wouldn't stop... Until the evening, when she phoned Auntie Anişoara and spoke with her and she sent me to visit her right away.

I remember it being almost night when I got there. I was barefoot. My mom wouldn't let me wear those azure blue shoes again, so I entered my auntie's house without taking any shoes off.

It was obvious she was shocked, too, but she tried to hide it. She gave me some sweets and then she gave me a pair of new socks and she invited me to the bathroom to wash and I did, and then, with motherly care my auntie mended my wounds and put the new socks on my feet.

"You look much better", she said to me smiling, and I couldn't help to remember that she was a kindergarten teacher, but then she said suddenly:

"The real present is not the socks, but these shoes", and a moment later she handed me a mocha brown and slightly heavy shoe box.

"Mihai, your cousin, wore these shoes when he entered high school", she whispered. I opened the box eagerly. There the shoes were, in very good condition.

How ever happy I was, that fact still remained that they were used shoes. But I took them and put them on, and they were my size, comfortable shoes.

Back home I asked my mother for pitch black leather paint and a thin brush. I repainted the shoes back to their original color and let them dry. The next day was an exciting morning. I put them on and rushed to school where I had a rehearsal for a play I was in, only to hear my teacher, Roxana Braga, the young and extremely beautiful wife of Braga, the writer, exclaim: "Nice new shoes, you got there, Florin!", and I couldn't tell if she really thought they were nice or she was mocking me for wearing someone else's old shoes. Anyway, it wasn't the first time I had to suffer because of my rare foot size. A few winters before, my sister got a new pair of skating boots for Christmas. White. They shined like the blade they were carrying underneath, and while they did, I couldn't help wanting a pair for myself too.

The plan was that we both would get skating boots that Christmas but my mom could't find my size. But when I was already giving up hope, my dad put an announcement in the local newspaper, so one or our friends saw it and called us to tell us that a neighbor of his had a daughter and that she had had skating boots when she was in Junior High School. So my parents took a present to those strangers and asked them to sell them, if they still had them, to us, and they were nice people and took the money. So, like in a fairytale story before January ended I started to skate awkwardly beside my already experienced sister. We had some very nice winters back in the 80's and we used to skate on frozen ponds or icy roads, and we stopped only then we had outgrown the boots, and we never got others to replace them. Those were the times. So years later, my mom gave our skating boots to Vasile's daughter and they used them for a couple of weeks before their father traded them for booze. Pufoaică brandy perhaps, I'm not sure.

I hope you can understand how frustrated I was with shoes in communism. That was the reason I said what I wanted from our new freedom was to get a decent pair of shoes. Nothing more, nothing less. And I got the following year a new pair of white sneakers. The first and the last until 1994. I was living then in a rented apartment in Sibiu. My father wanted me to live close to my new High School. But we were terribly poor. We had trouble finding money to pay the rent and prices were skyrocketing. So I had to go to school every day with my one and only pair of sneakers and they got so many holes in them that my socks were visible from several different angles. Only when I graduated did my father buy me a new pair of buckskin brown leather dress shoes, but, then he died, and because that pair was the best pair we had in our house, we decided he should wear them on his final journey. God curse Iliescu and his men forever. Hungry people are never free, hungry people are always easy to manipulate, hungry people can't even die in their own shoes, and this was the "freedom" we had after 1989.

Back upstairs, after crying, I found my dad and The Colonel absorbed in the story of the Revolution. The news was that the military unit that had Ceaușescu as prisoner was under heavy attack. The brave soldiers of our motherland were defending it with their lives and Ceaușescu couldn't possibly escape.

"I'm sure they'd rather put a bullet in his head than let him leave with the terrorists", said The Colonel, and my half drunk father approved with a loud burp.

The fact is that the sound made by the gas gathered in my father's stomach was louder than all the noises combined in and around Targoviste military base where Ceaușescu was held. Nobody was attacking it, so Kamenici couldn't wait anymore. His nails were already gone, anyway. Somebody had to attack them. It was Ceaușescu or him, General Voinea's threat was there, in his head, so somebody had to attack them.

It was early evening when somebody fired a shot, a single shot at their building. And all hell broke loose. Every soldier took their gun to the windows and started to fire outside the compound. Nobody was firing at them but that wasn't the important thing. The important thing was that everybody believed that they were being attacked, as the TV said, by superior forces.

He ran towards the room where Ceaușescu and his wife were being held and shouted:

"These headquarters are being overrun. Kill them and fall back to defensive positions. Save yourselves!"

Those that got the orders were major Ion Boboc and lieutenant-major Iulian Stoica. The first of them would remember years later:

"It was about 5:00p.m. when something happened. A diversion, I think. Somebody fired towards our positions from the high school across the road. At that moment everybody started to shoot. It was hell on earth. People were shooting from offices, hallways, the dorms upstairs, and us, being inside, we had the impression that a battle was taking place inside the building. But the reality is that nobody was shooting but us. So the commander came and gave that order and left. A few moments later everybody deserted the headquarters. Left behind were only me, Stoica and the two Ceaușescus. I didn't want to kill them so I got out of the room. The place was deserted. Silent. Everybody was outside in defensive positions. There were phones ringing, but nobody to pick them up or to ask what to do? So I looked outside and saw two soldiers with their guns pointed towards the headquarters' doors and I realized what it was all about. After executing Ceaușescu we were to be shot for not defending the prisoners, or for deserting. And they would have said that Ceaușescu was killed by strangers that entered the headquarters during that confused battle.

So I didn't go out. We waited there, and in one hour everybody was back, working as if nothing had happened".

But the reality is that the trap was more evil than Boboc first thought. That was because he only heard Kamenici shouting the order while he was in the room with Ceaușescu and his wife.

Stoica was outside the room, and he got another order, a direct and whispered one:

"The headquarters are lost, in the enemy's hands. Put an AKM clip in Ceauşescu and one in Elena".

"Then he left me. But the next day on 25th he accused me of treason. Because I didn't execute his order. I didn't do it and that was smart because a friend, an officer, had been ordered to open fire with the 14.5mm heavy machine gun on the room holding Ceauşescu if he heard gunshots from inside. 'Flatten the building', was the order" confessed Stoica in 1994 in front of the "1989 Commission".

So, The Colonel was right! Someone was definitely ready to put a bullet in Ceauşescu's head before handing him over to the nonexistent terrorists, but his imagination was, as you see, very poor. He recognized this, during a house party, just weeks before my father died, and he said that we were all wrong, we did a very bad thing to kill Ceauşescu like a pig, on Christmas Day.

Actually I didn't think that, at the time. I was twenty and still very young, and still very upset at my lack of decent shoes during and after communism, but when I got older and saw how decently the Iraqi people treated Saddam Hussein, how well conducted his trial was, I bowed in respect. Then I knew that we had been worse than animals in 1989, or at least those who took power in Romania were worse than animals. They wanted money, they wanted power, but they did nothing for the hungry people. For the starving bodies they destroyed all of Romania's agriculture favoring GMO foods imported from the West. And for starving minds they prepared sex, cheap TV dramas, Latin American telenovelas, Sandra Brown's books and mind-numbingly stupid variety shows.

The Colonel was already drunk when he got into his ABI to leave. We saw him to the gate, me, my sister, my father and my mother. Our grandmother was already asleep, not interested in political change.

"These are for you", he said to my mom and he gave her 6 military cans of beef. "They are war supplies. We took them all. Let us just hope the fucking Russians don't attack us, because in that event our soldiers will have nothing to eat", he said, and he climbed in the Jeep-like ABI, and those two soldiers waiting for him were as drunk as he was, but that didn't matter, coz the ABI's engine came to life and the car rolled away into the night. As usual in my town, lacking street lights, it was pitch dark. It was a moonless night, and we couldn't see the stars. Clouds were gathering. But from every house there were fairytale lights. There were the candles burning on the Christmas trees, and the trees were placed as usual so they could be seen from outside. They were all beautiful, and the town itself was beautiful and that was the first time that day I felt like it was Christmas Eve. We all felt it so we went inside and knocked on my grandmother's door, and woke her up. My mom brought to her first floor room Christmas fruitcakes, sweets and warm milk for everyone. Coffee for my father and we all ate and sung carols and talked like a family. We were waiting for the young men from town to come and sing their traditional carols so that we would all know it's Christmas. Lord Jesus was about to come again into the world as a baby, and we were all there to celebrate it. That was more important than the revolution continuing in the blaring Opera TV set upstairs, more important than our life without decent shoes.

Christmas was a magical time. It was the day after Ignat's Day that all young men and women, which means everyone over 15 years old, gathered in packs. Each street had its own pack, or, in places with shorter streets, a few blocks had their own pack. All these packs had names. Ancient names. Names from times when communism wasn't yet invented by Marx. Like Pietrari, the Stone Masons. They were from a street not very far from ours. But nobody, not even the old people, ever remember anyone there in the stone business. And these packs would go to a host family, and they would sing carols, pray and do other small preparations. Fasting was required and of course everybody dressed in traditional white clothes. Girls with pitch black skirts and vests, boys with those white sheepskin vests embroidered in red, made by my grandmother.

It was nightfall on the 24th they were waiting for. And it was already the 24th.

"Are they coming?" my mom asked anxiously.

"Yep", replied my father, quite satisfied. "Christmas cannot start without their carols. The Revolution asked them, however, to be decent this year, because many people have died and we should mourn them. So there won't be any meteleauă this year".

He hadn't finished when I was already gasping for air. Meteleauă was my favorite festival. It was the winter number one event and was supposed to happen on the 28th. It was like a carnival. The boys in each pack would dress up as something funny and, usually drunk, they paraded through the town. They were supposed to do stupid things to keep away devils, and they were so funny. Meteleauă was also a process of initiation. The young child would get drunk for the very first time and would parade through the entire city as a man should, with his head up, proud, and his mom and dad would wave from the crowd and he would know that he was a man, and everyone would treat him like he was a man, from then on. So he would stop greeting everybody with sărut-mâna or "I kiss your hand" and would say "Hello" or "Good day" instead.

No more meteleauă was news as sad as no Christmas presents. But as we were waiting there, my mom started to smile and said:

"I heard something upstairs. You kids go and check under the Christmas tree. Perhaps it was Father Christmas", and she didn't have time to finish her sentence. We rushed past her and went straight to the Christmas tree, and yes, something was waiting there for us. Our presents were light and we opened them eagerly. Each of us had a handmade woollen set of hat, muffler, gloves and socks. Mine were royal blue and my sister's were scarlet. There were some chocolates too.

"We love you, mommy", we both cried out, and rushed to her and dad. And all that I saw on their faces was pure happiness.

Only today, after so many years, do I realize that she must have stayed awake into the night making those woollen winter clothes for us and I realize how difficult it must have been for her, and I love her for it. I also love my father for his support. That present was the most beautiful present I ever got for Christmas. I was sure I would get nothing, but I got something which was more valuable than all the things that our looted and destroyed bookstore offered, or all the things that the revolution brought us in hypermarkets.

We were already downstairs, new hats and new socks on when we heard the young men singing for our neighbor. Next it was our turn. So we waited. And we heard the gate opening and then closing and many many footsteps gathering before our door. Then, those 30 or so young men started to sing as loud as they could "Joseph and Mary" and that carol literally crashed against our chests and our bodies, and hearts got to know that it was Christmas.

My father started to cry and I realized that he never had cried when we listened to that carol before, when my grandfather was still with us. "Why are you crying?" I once asked him and he said he cried because he was the oldest in our family, that he remembered how it was when he was in the pack, singing those beautiful carols, and he cried because he was the next man in our family to die.

I swear to God, I was so young when he talked with me about why he cried when he listened to that carol that I couldn't really understand him. I tried to, but it felt so strange to cry at that very happy moment. Only years later, in 1995, when my father had been buried 10 months, I started to cry the very moment the words "Joseph and Mary" hit my chest, and I cried like my father did and like my grandfather did before him, knowing everything my father used to know, and my grandmother was dead too. Only my mother, my sister, and I were left. We gave the young men money for their performance, because money was everything those days. Money had become more important than life.

However, back in 1989 we gave the young men the sweet cheese cake that my mom made for them and a kilo of smoked ham. That particular ham we made from the pig's muscles situated along the back bone. It was kept in salt for one day and smoked for another two. We used to eat it raw if smoked more than 10 days. It was still fresh so the young men had to fry it before thrusting it into their stomachs. We also gave them 100 lei, the same amount that Ceauşescu promised everybody in his last speech.

The following year was to be the last year people gave those sweet cakes and meat to the carol singers. Romania wasn't starving anymore and imported meat was available in food stores all the time. The young men didn't fast and those cakes and the meat they got they couldn't eat. So when they got drunk they had food fights with the bread and meat, and threw it in the snow, and the old people saw it, and we all just stopped giving those traditional gifts. And they got only money, until Romania entered the European Union in 2004 and young people migrated in mass to work in construction, as babysitters, as dishwashers and cleaning toilets for our wealthier European brothers and entire streets were left without their young people's packs. I heard that the heads of families still cry. The only difference is that they cry not because they are hit with the lyrics of "Joseph and Mary", but because there are no lyrics to hit them. No carols, except those re-mixed modern carols coming out of not old black and white, but new color TV sets. Merry Christmas, Romania, wherever you are!

It was already early when we went to bed, leaving, as customary, the gate open. That was for carol singers, whoever they were. Also sometimes friends or relatives came, even at three or four in the morning. But my father called it a day. He was sure that on that particular night, when the good people of Romania and its soldiers under the command of Iliescu, were battling terrorists and vicious forces of the former regime, we would have no visitors. So I got into my warm bed in which my mother had placed as usual at my feet a fire heated ceramic tile wrapped in towels. That would keep warm for hours, and I happily welcomed sleep. I was free, I had a happy and loving family, and I had nothing to fear. The only thing ahead was

Christmas Day, the most peaceful and full of love day of the year.

Strange as it is, those warm feelings of love and peace were utterly absent from Colonel Kamenici's head in Targoviste. Not that he was dead or he wasn't capable of feeling love and peace. He could, but not on that bloody night. He was still cursing Boboc and Stoica for their lack of guts. Why didn't those two suckers kill Nicolae and Elena? He could't understand it. His orders were clear. At least clearer than those he gave to Tecu and Mares on the morning of the 23rd. Why the hell did them sons-of-bitches not comply?

"It's you or him! You got it?" "You are finished". "Only one of you will survive this Revolution alive". The words of General Voinea, the head of the First Army, were banging ever louder in his head.

Half an hour later, as if his prayers had been answered by the God he didn't believe in, their unit was attacked with gunfire from the north. So he took a TAB and drove it to the tanks' positions where he had a long discussion with the tanks commander, lieutenant-colonel Mutu.

"How many tanks could he count on if they were to take the two Ceauşescus in a march to Bucharest?" was his question. "Sixteen" was the answer.

"And, if we are attacked on our way there?" he asked again.

"Then we will stop, group the tanks together and fight", was the answer.

"And, if we are outnumbered and overpowered?" he asked again and lieutenant-colonel Mutu said calmly:

"Then we kill Ceauşescu."

Twenty years after that night we can only guess that that plan wasn't pursued because it was impossible to overpower 16 heavy TR-80 Army Tanks. To overpower them one had to have 16 brand new soviet tanks or 20 brand new Abraham tanks, and it wasn't likely the invisible terrorists could get their hands on heavier artillery.

Maybe that was the reason why the two Ceauşescus didn't spend their last night in military beds, as they had spent the two nights before, but seated inside a TAB armored personnel carrier, along with their impossibly stinky and sleepy guards.

Kamenici ordered Nicolae and Elena to get in a TAB. They would be in danger, if the headquarters were stormed by hostile forces. First they didn't want to but they had to comply. With them, their guards Stoica and Boboc and another one, an officer with Tragoviste's Militia. The driver was a civilian. Those were the times. The Army started to fight for the people and not against them so they had to welcome civilians that wanted to lend a hand, not that they were in any need of civilians there. So the TAB started its noisy engine to start its heater and everybody tried to sleep while they waited for morning.

But that TAB wasn't the only one with a running engine there. Behind it was another one and in this one Kamenici was waiting. He had with him lieutenant-colonel Dinu, and as a driver he had private Stoican; another one, named Birtan was holding an AKM. There was a radio man and another soldier. It wasn't crowded, but they all started to breathe easy when Kamenici went out for a smoke, everybody thought. But as Kamenici was smoking he called his driver.

Many years after that night, private Stoican recalled:

"Kamenici was smoking. He was wearing a pufoaică". It was the same kind of winter coat that was turned into alcohol after being dipped in urine and shit by the Revolution-loving Romanian people.

"He had his hands in his pockets, and he asked me:"

"You, you know who's in that TAB?"

"So what could I possibly say? So I said:"

"Sir, I heard something but I can't be sure, sir!"

"And he told me:"

"If you want a place in the history books, go over there and shoot them both".

Stoican was trying to control his fear when Kamenici went to the TAB holding Ceauşescu and pulled the driver out. He told the man he was a civilian and it was Christmas Eve.

"Go to your wife and kids, thank you for what you did for the Revolution, Merry Christmas and God bless you and your family" he said, and asked the reluctant Stoican to take his place.

"I didn't want to, but I had no power to say no. I was almost crying. I begged my commander to change his mind because I wasn't shaved and I couldn't present myself before our supreme commander in the shape I was in. But there I was inside. Kamenici had to push me to get me in, but once I was in the driver's seat I saw them. They were wearing military clothes and looked at me with bright eyes. Stoica and Boboc had guns on their knees but they were almost asleep. They tried to open their eyes but they were so tired that they couldn't. If Ceauşescu had wanted to take one of their guns he could have done it. Paisie however wasn't sleeping but his gun was sticking out a crenel (a shooting hole), and sometimes he would just speak with Ceauşescu".

Stoican was awake almost all night and so was Paisie and Ceauşescu. He tried to decide whether he should kill Ceauşescu and his wife or not.

"Should I kill them or should I not kill them?" that was his dilemma. He tried to find a reason for doing it or a reason for not doing it, but he couldn't come to a conclusion, so the morning found him unprepared and undecided.

In 1998 Iulian Stoica officially declared that Stoican confessed that night that his orders were to kill everyone in the TAB, and it made sense. Both Stoica and Boboc were the traitors that didn't follow similar orders the previous afternoon, weren't they? But all of them were still alive and an angry Colonel Kamenici called the mission off and invited the half frozen people into his headquarters and phoned Bucharest to report that Ceauşescu and his wife were alive and well and asked for advice. But the killing machine that had been created to assassinate Ceauşescu was already rolling, without his knowledge. A team was being put together at that very hour, and everything was to go as planned, the long transition, the economic crises were all about to begin.

5. DECEMBER 25TH

On Christmas Day I woke up at 4 am. Liviu, my godfather and his brother Dan, together with their young wives were singing carols at the top of their voices under our window. I only got up to greet them with the traditional "Merry Christmas" and went back my bed while my parents went down for an early breakfast with our unexpected guests.

Later that day my dad said that Dan looked like a ghost. He was worried about him but the reason behind those haunted eyes, that had scared my father, we found out only months later, when Dan was finally ready to talk.

When the Revolution started to spread on 22nd, Dan was at home in Odorheiu Secuiesc. That small and beautiful city, where my mother's cousin was married to a Hungarian, had a majority Hungarian population. Romanians were few. Some, like my mother's cousin were teachers at the school, teaching Romanian as a foreign language to the local kids, others like Dan were working in the Army, Police or Securitate. Although the local

Communist Party Organization was almost 100% Hungarian, the local folks somehow perceived the Romanians as "dictator lovers" so for them the local Revolution was more a Revolution against Romanians.

Dan was at his job that morning when he sensed the danger and decided it was time to get his young wife out of town before it was too late, and decided it was best for them to flee in a military truck. They were packing when the revolutionaries marched from the local factories where they worked to the City Hall to take over. Thousands of people marching in unison, shouting in Hungarian anti-Ceauşescu slogans.

That was the image that Dan's best friend, a Hungarian, saw when he suddenly realized that people would recognize Dan's car, parked so close to the City Hall, as a car driven by a Romanian. The number plates said it all. They were from an area with very few Hungarians, so he had to be quick. He smashed a window and got in. He tried to start it by connecting wires as he had once seen in some American movie, but people from the steadily closing march started to run towards the car. They knew the car! They could see the license plates!

In a second Dan's best friend was surrounded. He tried to get out and talk some sense into those workers, to tell them there was no need to vandalize that car, his friend's car, but he was punched in the head through the broken window. He tried again, but there were already too many people around the car and they started to hit him as they turned the Dacia upside down.

He was confused when they did that and, because he wasn't wearing a seat belt, was on the car's ceiling trying to figure out how to best get out of the car but also the best way to get away from the boots that were trying to reach him through the shattered windows. He still wasn't afraid. He believed he would get out eventually, so he was more sorry for Dan's car than for himself. But then he could smell it and let out a scream. And he screamed until the flames of the torched car entered his lungs, and kicked, trying to get out and got kicked by heavy boots and...

People were already leaving when Dan went to pick up his car to park it inside the military unit and he saw it was burning. He wanted to leave immediately but something had caught his eye, so he casually walked towards the car until he was standing beside it and could look inside. It was there. That leather jacket that his friend had bought from Hungary last summer. There were no other jackets like that in the whole of Romania and that burning jacket was on something that was definitely human. His eyes started to fill with tears, for the first time in so many years. He hadn't cried since his mom died when he was still a child, but he was crying then. He felt the world falling apart and started to run, to get away.

The first victim of the Revolution in Odorheiu Secuiesc was a Good Samaritan. But the second was not. The second was the head of the local branch of Securitate, and the people who killed him took his head out of the building they had set on fire and played football with it. What a happy mood there was, communism was collapsing and they were using their freedom for what western people usually use it: leisure!

But at four in the morning on Christmas Day I was oblivious to all that. I didn't know that Kamenici was still waiting in his TAB to hear shots in the other. I didn't know that the most mysterious man of the Romanian Revolution, Gelu Voican Voiculescu, the same one that was about to become Romania's Ambassador to Tunisia, was assembling the men who were about to judge Ceauşescu in a kangaroo court.

Iliescu himself signed a decree on December 22nd, minutes after he got confirmation that Ceauşescu had been captured. I didn't know that 20 years after people and journalists would still be debating whether that signature was valid or not, whether Iliescu was officially the head of the new power or whether he was still   just the head of the Technical Publishing House.

So I was innocent in my sleep and, when I woke up for the second time that morning it was already 10:00am. My mother used to let me sleep in during holidays. I often stayed up reading books way past midnight. Liviu, Dan and their young, beautiful wives were already gone and our gate was closed. Christmas Day was a day when nobody went out, so nobody came to visit. Christmas Day was a day when even the Church was closed. The

Christmas mass started and ended before the roosters rang in the morning at 8, so why bother keeping the gate open all day long?

In the kitchen I refused breakfast, favoring, as always on Christmas, fruitcakes, cakes and cookies. I was washing everything down with a mug of hot milk – my mom was there so cold milk wasn't an option – when my father announced the day's schedule.

"Today they're gonna kill Ceaușescu, and I plan on watching it. Let's go all upstairs and play Scrabble or a card game of twist, sing carols and watch the television".

Now that was a first. We usually stayed in my grandmother's room and listened to her stories. Before that we used to listen to my grandfather's stories, and they were so interesting.

My grandmother had interesting stories too. Her best one was about when her sister died. She was with her, in her final moments.

"Floare", she said to my grandmother, and that's "Flower" in Romanian.

"Floare, can you see that white dove on the stove?" her dying sister asked.

"No, my dear, there's no white pigeon on the stove!" my grandmother replied.

"Oh, Floare, you can't see it because He didn't come for you. He said that you still have to wait. But He's here for me. The Holy Spirit, Floare, the Holy Spirit! He's here for my soul. God bless you too." she had said and her soul was taken, probably by a white bird that waited for her on the hot stove, to say goodbye. It was the year I was born, 1975, during the winter. And the bird was right, my grandmother, despite being the first born, had to wait for it another nineteen long years.

So there we were, half watching TV, playing Scrabble with my unbeatable father and listening to carols. My grandmother only came for a couple of hours, she went to her room. She didn't like the TV and the news it spread. On Christmas one had to think about the miracle of Nativity not about people being shot.

"The world is going to end. People killing each other in the Holy Week of Christmas, nothing good will come out of this!"

she half shouted and left, leaving my father and me smiling. We were the idiots. We smiled believing that grandmother was too old but the fact remains, she was the only one that got it right.

But in less than five minutes my grandmother was back with terrible news. Our neighbor, Comrade Stoica, a devoted party member who really believed in communism despite living in a huge house that others could not afford, had died. He was really young, not even 40, but even more terrible was the news that he had died with his wife and youngest son. The old ladies' network was functioning and my grandmother said she would go with candles to mourn them and invited my parents too. Eventually they went the next day, shocked.

"I hope they didn't commit suicide", my father said. "Ceaușescu doesn't deserve such gratitude." And he was probably referring to the Japanese General Nogi, the same one that visited Romania and befriended our queen who committed suicide with his wife after his Meiji Emperor died.

"No, God take care of their pure souls", they died in an accident. You know last night was windy, and they took a bath, after listening to the 'Joseph and Mary' carol. It was carbon monoxide. The wind had pushed the exhaust gases back into the bathroom and they didn't stand a chance, my grandmother told us. She was already candles in hand, going to give the news to other old women in town. How sad Christmas had suddenly become. Three days later their funeral was the talk of the town. The young men that sang to them their last 'Joseph and Mary' went deep into the forest and cut a huge pine tree. It wasn't a Christmas tree but a tree with which the boy that died that night would be married during the funeral for the afterlife. We always planted pines on the graves of unmarried boys, but nobody wished to plant one that particular Christmas. The people hated communism but cried when they took the three bodies to the graveyard. Comrade Stoica was a good communist and he had only friends. No enemies.

With grandmother gone mourning and our games canceled because of the sad news, time was passing slowly. For me, for my family, but not for Ceaușescu. Or for his soon-to-be killers. The trial started at 1:20 pm not long after Nicolae and his wife had had their meal. Should they have known that would be their last one, maybe they would have appreciated it, despite the fact that it was meager. Not that Ceauşescu ate only French cuisine every day. He ate French cuisine on occasion but he was still a peasant's son, so he often ate like farmers, white bread with cheese and tomatoes. Except the bread and tomatoes he used to eat were fresh, and the cheese was handmade and didn't have that metallic taste added to it when it was processed by the state-owned dairy industry.

Now, there's a big chance you saw this trial on TV. With subtitles. Ceauşescu didn't take it seriously. How could he? He was accused of killing 60,000 people in Timişoara, of destroying and damaging buildings with explosions in cities, the destruction of the Romanian economy, and attempting to escape from Romania with more than one billion dollars in foreign bank accounts. That trial was insane. Senile as he was, he had been loosing it in his final years, he definitely thought it was a joke. It had to be. If his army killed 60,000 as his wife Elena had ordered, then he was supposed to be enjoying lunch at his office, as usual, not detained for the last three days. And by who? By Iliescu. He knew that Iliescu had been eyeing the role of Romania's Gorbachev, but he had believed that wasn't going to happen. And the things about the economy they had said. Romania was the only country in the world with no foreign debt. Romania was poor but independent and he had just been pressuring Iran and Libia to finance, with their oil, a new International Monetary Fund for poor countries.

That trial was a joke. At least when he was arrested by the king's police before Romania turned into a communist state, his defenders did their job and defended him. Now, at his second trial more than 40 years later his defense, a man called Lucescu and another called Teodorescu, were accusing him as much as the prosecutors. What the fuck?! He was nervous. He could feel his wife was nervous too. There had to be a way to solve this civilly, like the people in East Germany or in Czeckhoslovakia had. He was trying to think of what he could offer in exchange for his freedom, when his trial ended, as suddenly as it had started. It was 2:40 pm. The trial had lasted only an hour and 20 minutes.

The judges left to deliberate but even that deliberation was a joke. They hadn't even finished their smokes properly when they were ordered back inside to read the verdict.

Death by execution! It was 2:45 pm. The sentence was to be executed immediately, they said. Not even in Ceauşescu's Romania was it possible to kill people so easily. Romania, a dictatorship as it was, still had laws. People respected them and, when they didn't there were trials. But even mock trials lasted longer. And the accused had the right to appeal. Not since the end of WWII and the communist purges had people been shot like animals.

Twenty years later I am happy for the Iraqi people. They had the chance to send Saddam to hell in an organized way. There was a trial and the trial didn't finish in 80 minutes. And Saddam, if compared with Ceauşescu, was indeed a criminal. The genocides he was accused of were real. But in Romania more people died after Ceauşescu was captured than when he was in power.

I know now, twenty years on, that not one of those who ordered people killed in Bucharest, at Universitate Square or at the airport or at the Ministry of Defense, were prosecuted. Nobody ended up behind bars. General Stănculescu got a prison term, but only 18 years later, and he was out in almost no time. "What are you doing here, General?", he was asked when he was found in a casino by the media. "Killing time", was his answer.

After being sentenced to death, Ceauşescu didn't have any time left to kill. Or to think. He was taken and despite his protests his hands were tied behind his back. He wanted to go in a dignified way.

"You're hurting me! I raised you as I raised my own kids", Elena was screaming at the soldiers who were ordered to tie her hands, but they didn't care. Everybody felt it was about time to end it all and looked forward to the promised freedom.

Ceauşescu and Elena were dragged out of that room and a few meters away put against a wall.

"He's first, then you!", somebody informed Elena.

"No way! We fought together, we die together!" she said and she showed more dignity than all the men in uniform in Targoviste's military base.

Ceauşescu started to sing the The Internationale (the communist anthem), but when he heard the AKM's being armed he shouted:

"Long live the free and independent Socialist Republic of Romania". And then he died. It was 2:50 pm. Nobody organized a firing squad, nobody gave the order to fire! The soldiers started to shoot and nobody could tell who was first. They fell on their backs, eyes wide open gazing at the sky. At least they were able to refuse the black blindfolds.

The fact is that the execution was so poorly organized that the cameraman brought especially from Romanian National Television by Gelu Voican Voiculescu didn't record it! He was about to change the batteries when Ceauşescu was sent to meet the white dove my grandmother's sister saw on her death bed. He got closer when the firing stopped and filmed the face that every single Romanian wanted to see that Christmas Day, their dead Ceauşescu, but there was not much to film. Blood was coming out of his nose and just he looked like all dead people usually look. My father didn't look much better when he died, five years and four months later in 1995.

It was a nice spring day but he didn't feel so good and went home. He said to my mom that he would lie down for an hour or so, but when she checked on him he was unresponsive. Dr. Rogojan, the same old doctor that we asked to come in the middle of the night and paid a 100 lei came, and he simply announced, "Coma!". Did nothing to my father, took his pay, doubled many times by the skyrocketing inflation of those years and called the ambulance. After he called it he went on his way, and my sister called me.

I cannot say whether I was lucky or unlucky. I was living in Bucharest then, studying Journalism at the University and experiencing first love in the arms of Cosmina, a girl that wanted to be a babe, from my high school in Sibiu. I had no phone, no mobile phone, no pager. So my sister called Ms. Jenny, a 60 year old widow living next door, and she came and knocked on my door and I was there.

"Come immediately, father is unconscious, we're waiting for the ambulance to take him to Sibiu", she said, and I started to run and I went into the subway without paying. I had no money to spare. I was only hoping the train prices hadn't changed since the week before when I visited my family and didn't say "I love you!" to my father, as I have should have.

But I was quite lucky that day to get the afternoon train. There were only three trains every day for Sibiu, one in the morning, another in the afternoon and the last one, a night train, so I was lucky to get it. It was crowded. Those days people still used trains to travel and I stood in the corridor and when I cried I opened the window to let the wind dry my tears.

"Please God, not him!" I was saying all the time, but over and over I was remembering how, the previous night, while studying in the National Library, suddenly some poetry had entered my head and I wrote it down, reading it after without understanding it's meaning.

"I sniff, I sniff in the air/ The smell of death and despair/ I sniff the Occidental wind/ And shout, I know death is wind/ And sliced myself in two big halves/ One for Hell and one for Gods/ I sniff, I sniff in the air/ The smell of death and despair"!

But I couldn't sense what was waiting for me in Avrig. Uncle Lulu was at the train station with his car, waiting. That was a first. Nobody ever waited for me at the train station, not even when I went as a child, every day, by myself to Sibiu with a broken arm, for rehabilitation.

So I expected my father was already dead, but Uncle Lulu said that he wasn't. So I started to hope, only to reach home and see all my relatives there, all the aunties and uncles and cousins, all sweeping the front yard, cleaning the house, preparing it for the funeral.

They were either lying to me or they weren't giving my dad a single chance.

Only a long time after that day did I understand the drama of my father's death. He was executed after being judged and sentenced by people who were more ruthless than those that killed Ceauşescu.

The Ambulance came a half an hour after Dr. Rogojan called. They looked at my father and waited for my mother to tip them generously. But we were poor. We had no money. The money that we had went to paying my studies and my one bedroom apartment in Bucharest. So, when they saw that there was nothing to take, they took my father with them. My mom wanted to ride in the ambulance, too, but they said it wasn't allowed. We'll take him to the City Central Hospital", they had said and, through the closing door, they gave my mom my father's wedding ring.

"Lady, you wanna keep that. If he dies and is put in the morgue before you get there, they'll steal it!", they said and closed the door in the disorientated face of my mom. So what happened was that she panicked but had the strength to dial 23850, the phone number of my Uncle Ion, and she spoke with my cousin Ioan and asked him to go to the City Central coz my father was almost dead in an Ambulance with some heartless people beside him.

And she dressed in less than 3 minutes and still crying went out with the intention of hijacking a car, because we had no car, the train was hours away and a connecting bus with Sibiu was available only in the morning, once.

My cousin first finished his meal and then walked to the hospital. The ambulance had already returned from Avrig, he learned, and the man inside was on a bed in the hospital waiting for medical help.

But he couldn't enter the hospital, those were the rules, so he went and bought some flowers and some chocolates and gave them to a nurse and he smiled, and she smiled back and let him through. And he took the stairs because only the special elevator carrying people to and from the operating room was working, and only an hour and a half, after receiving that phone call from my mom did cousin Ioan finally get to see dad.

"The moment I entered the room, blood started to flow from your father's nose" he told me during the funeral, and I thanked him for being there. That piece of information was all that we needed to know. It meant that my father didn't die alone, like an animal, but died like all human beings should, with someone watching over them, telling them, "It's OK, you are not alone, you have a loving family beside you".

My mom got there but it was too late. And it was our own fault that we were poor and had no money to tip the people working in the Ambulance. We were too poor so that was why we were judged and then sentenced and then executed by our motherfucking country, this time Iliescu's country. Romania couldn't provide for us all. There were industries to be dismantled and sold for the benefit of the chosen few. The teachers and doctors and all other public servants were paid only meager wages. My father was a public servant but when he died he had no decent shoes. That was why we buried him in mine.

About 3000 people attended his funeral. He was young and he was popular. I was walking behind the horse led funeral carriage, and that funeral carriage was made of glass, and what I saw reflected in that unlikely mirror was the huge cortege of people walking behind me, my sister and my mom. There were enough of us for another Revolution, I thought, because 1989 was the last time so many people walked together through my town. The only difference was that my father wasn't at the front but the back and he wasn't being carried but walking with them.

In 1989, on 25th of December, we never imagined that that was the freedom we were getting when we listened to the news on the TV that Ceauşescu had been executed. It was Christmas Day and people were cheering like it was New Year's, or like Romania had just won the Soccer World Cup. We were quite happy and satisfied too.

"I'm so sorry grandfather didn't live to see this moment", my dad said, referring to his own father. "He just hated the fact that he shared his birthday with Ceauşescu, January 26th", he said, and he was repeating himself. The truth is that my grandfather had also said those words so many times during his final weeks that we started to fear political prosecutions for the entire family.

"Free Romanian Television", the new name of our one and only TV station, of course changed in the months following the Revolution to "Romanian Television", because it wasn't free, announced that we would see the trial and the execution. At that time other TV stations around the globe were already airing that macabre show. Some people in Romanian Television were already thinking of making money for themselves.

So we were just waiting around when dinner time came and my father said we should not eat in the kitchen but set the dining table in the middle of our room again, which we did. We took the fine tablecloth, which took my grandmother 3 months to make, and lit candles, and prepared everything like it was an anniversary. Fine crystal glasses replaced the usual ones, and my sister was allowed to take out our finest tableware and silverware. Even the wine I got from the basement I put it in a crystal carafe. It was all so exciting.

My mom brought as entrées caltaboși, tobă, cîrnaţi and sângerete, together with beef salad, a delicacy usually made with boiled chicken, because we didn't have beef. It also contained boiled vegetables, pickles and mayonnaise, stuffed eggs, eggplant salads, mushroom salad made with mayonnaise, garlic and white cottage cheese.

Everything was on the table when we heard some loud knocks at the gate. It was strange. People never visit on Christmas Day. It had to be something important.

I wanted to go and check it out, but my father went instead.

"Kids, set another place at the table and one more glass, coz we have a guest", my father said in a very strange tone of voice. And then, addressing that visitor:

"You are very lucky to arrive just now, because they are about to show us how Ceaușescu got killed".

Now, as they opened the door to come inside, I was half-shocked. I expected someone we knew, not a total strange. But, that man, whoever he was, was as shocked to see us, the entire family, including my grandmother, around that festive table.

"Please, sit down", said my father and his tone of voice wasn't the one that he used for happy events, but the one that he used when my sister presented him with bad grades. My father was worried.

"Let's eat, let's drink" he said as our unexpected and unknown guest sat at the table without removing his winter coat.

When I say "unknown" I mean that he wasn't from our town. We knew everybody, all 10,000 people living in Avrig but that man wasn't among them. That was really strange.

My father poured wine into the glasses, only a drop for grandmother and my mom, and I filled my glass and my sister's glass with herb tea. It was the only drink we knew except some very difficult to get orange juice and Pepsi Cola. Then, as we all sat down, my father raised his glass and said:

"Cheers! Let us drink to the freedom we got today, on Christmas Day. God has provided us with it and our kids will use this freedom right!" and everybody, including our strange guest repeated the toast.

"Let's eat!" someone said, but we were already attacking the homemade delicacies on the table. The bread we had that day was fresh and I understood that my grandmother had made it in our gas oven when she complained about the taste. It was great bread, white and soft, but she didn't like it. As usual when she made bread in the gas oven she complained about us destroying her wood burning oven, the same one that my grandfather had built for her - to her exact specifications.

She was old so we all said that the bread was great and that she should make it more often, and while we were eating my father and our visitor were getting slowly but inevitably drunk. Suddenly the footage of Ceaușescu's death was introduced and we all cheered and we watched it eating, like Americans with their popcorn in the movie theaters.

We saw and heard how the defense had joined the prosecution in accusing Ceaușescu and how they made him shut his mouth several times, but we didn't care. Ceaușescu on that screen was not a person, but my lack of decent shoes, he was the waiting in line in the morning for milk and in the afternoon for bread, he was the vegan diet that parents offered to their kids instead of a diet with eggs and meat, he was the cold inside the houses of those people living in flats, the cold water and lack of medication. Ceauşescu on that screen was the feeling we had when we didn't get oranges for Christmas, and every other small thing that we were not satisfied with.

The footage had been cut short, but in the end we all saw the bodies of Ceauşescu and Elena, and we happily exclaimed, "We are free, we are free". My mom started to cry, and also my grandmother, even if I suspect their reasons were different.

But so was our unknown winter-coat-clad visitor. He was drunker than my father was, maybe because he had decided to stay and eat and drink in a heated room with the kind of coat one would put on only when facing subzero temperatures. He was crying and my father was patting his shoulder, saying:

"It's over now, we are all free, we can all begin new lives", but the over-dressed stranger started to sob even louder. Then, he put his hand in his coat pocket and took out the first revolver I ever saw.

"Son", he said as he removed the bullets, "you might want to play with this".

I said "YEAH!", and took the gun. Curiously enough, in his hands it looked very light, but in mine it felt very heavy.

The stranger was wiping his eyes, when he said:

"Grancea, you have here a wonderful family, and you are a wonderful guy". My father just nodded.

"See", the stranger said, "it took me years to find out who my wife's first man was, because when I realized after my marriage that she wasn't pure, I swore I would kill that man with my own hands. I wanted to come here and kill you yesterday, but I saw a military car parked outside, so I postponed it till now."

He started to laugh.

"In Revolutions, people get killed and nobody asks questions, so that's why I came here today. But you are a nice guy, you invited me to your table, and offered me your wine, and we all ate food and drank it, and when I wanted to do it I just thought that we are actually friends. I love you, Grancea!" he said to my father and took my father by his shoulders and started to hug him. "I love you, șogore", he said, using a Hungarian word that I didn't understand.

Only years later someone told me that șogori are symbolic brothers united by the fact that they have loved the same woman. That's when I understood also why my mom was so upset after she heard that and why she picked on my father for months after. I understood but I didn't want to judge. Because on that evening I became a man, a man that learned that not always, and not all, drunk people are bad, a man that learned we can forgive even while we don't forget, a man that saw that a given hand is also a taken one, and that old foes can drink together and cry together. The man I had become that evening, unlike the boy that I was, believed in Father Christmas, because somehow Father Christmas was there with us and that over-coated stranger.

The end!

ABOUT THE AUTHOR

Florin lives in Japan with his family and continues to study the Romanian transition to democracy, the mass media and journalism.

19088685R00080

Made in the USA
Lexington, KY
06 December 2012